Grace Rose Farm

GARDEN
ROSES

Grace Rose Farm

GARDEN ROSES

The Complete Guide to
Growing & Arranging Spectacular Blooms

GRACIELINDA POULSON

Artisan | New York

Library of Congress Cataloging-in-Publication Data is on file.

ISBN 978-1-64829-083-1

Cover and book design by Shubhani Sarkar

Published by Artisan, an imprint of Workman Publishing,
a division of Hachette Book Group, Inc.
1290 Avenue of the Americas, New York, NY 10104
artisanbooks.com

The Artisan name and logo are registered trademarks of
Hachette Book Group, Inc.

Printed in China on responsibly sourced paper
First printing, February 2024

10 9 8 7 6 5 4 3 2 1

CONTENTS

INTRODUCTION

GARDEN ROSES HAVE ALWAYS EVOKED precious memories for me. Spending time with my grandma in her rose garden when I was young, I discovered that growing and clipping roses for others was my love language. As an adult, I wanted to try my hand at growing some myself. Collecting roses quickly became an obsession, and my backyard soon overflowed with five hundred bushes. When florists caught wind of my unique heirloom-inspired garden roses from my social media posts, that passion bloomed into a thriving business. My husband, Ryan, and I bought more plants and eventually more land to keep up with the demand. I went from growing roses as a hobbyist to producing thousands of blooms a year for my business, Grace Rose Farm, in Southern California. Now we work with breeders from around the world to bring new rosebushes to American gardeners and farm our own roses for weddings, events, and local flower lovers. We're also growing our online business, which delivers roses to customers around the country through partnerships with breeders and growers.

Over the years, I've been asked countless questions about rose care. For as popular as the rose is, it still intimidates so many, who fear its reputation as fickle and difficult to grow. That could not be further from the truth. I do not have a horticultural, biology, or agricultural background, yet I have successfully grown tens of thousands of rosebushes and harvested millions of gorgeous blooms from my bushes. Whether you're a novice or an experienced gardener, through trial and error and an open mind, your own beautiful rose garden can and will take shape.

The possibilities are endless when it comes to designing the rose garden of your dreams: There are thousands of varieties to choose from, and knowing where to begin can be overwhelming. In this book I will take you on a journey through roses—breaking down the bloom types, shapes, and fragrances you can choose from, and then introducing you to my favorite varieties, ones that can thrive in the home garden and bring you magnificent flowers year after year. Through chapters on planning your garden, planting, year-round rose care, harvesting, and arranging, you will learn the ins and outs of growing and enjoying roses. Roses are not difficult flowers—they simply require an investment of time and care. There are moments in the garden when toil and beauty collide, where you find that sweet place and you know it's worth all the effort to make your rose garden dream come true.

Whether you are trying your hand at gardening for the first time or are looking to expand your horizons, whether you have just a small patio or a spacious property, growing roses is possible if you're willing to learn. Surrounding yourself with beauty begins here.

Part One

TRIED-
AND-TRUE
ROSES

CHAPTER ONE

The

ESSENCE

of

ROSES

The world of roses is vast, and it can be a bit
overwhelming to choose the best varieties for your garden.
Knowing the differences between the types of roses will
help you narrow down those that match your experience
level, your intention for your flowers, the space your
garden allows for cutting or climbing roses, your desired
fragrance and preferred color palette, and more.

UNDERSTANDING ROSES

ROSES VARY GREATLY ACROSS VARIETIES. SOME HAVE CUPPED blooms and relatively few petals, while others are quartered and packed with more than one hundred petals. Additionally, each rose variety can encompass more than one "type" of bloom form. Here are some terms to familiarize yourself with before you dive into the world of rose gardening.

ROSE ANATOMY

Button Eye (1): Small petals that are curled over in the center of blooms

Bud (2): The unopened flower of a rose

Spray (3): A cluster of blooms branching off a cane

Leaflet (4): The collection of leaves, usually three to five, on a single leaf branch

Bud Eye (5): The swelling between a leaflet and cane where new growth occurs

Cane (6): A branch that grows from the base of the plant (main cane) or a lateral branch growing from a main cane

Crown (7): The base of the plant where roots and canes meet. Note: the bud union is here in grafted roses.

Stamen (8): The part of the rose that produces pollen, found within the center of the bloom

Sepals (9): Green leaves that protect the bloom in its bud form and open to reveal the petals as they unfurl. Roses have five sepals.

BLOOM FORMS

Cupped
Petals are formed in a rounded pattern, resulting in a curved shape that reveals a ruffled mass of interior petals in the center.

Flat
Petals appear to open fully outward, resulting in a flat, feathered-out shape. (Note: At the end of their bloom cycle, most roses, regardless of their bloom form, will open to be relatively flat.)

Globular
Petals fold upon each other in a tight, scalloping pattern, concealing the stamens and creating a sphere-like bloom form.

High-Centered
Outer petals open outward as inner petals stand tall in the center.

Old-Fashioned
Also known as cabbage-shaped, old-fashioned bloom forms feature petals that form in a ruffling, plentiful display. The bloom is cupped at the base and opens loosely in the center.

Pompon
A round head brimming with layer upon layer of petals. The outer petals curve in dramatically, giving way to a tight, ruffled view of the center.

Quartered
These blooms are packed with petals, creating folded quadrants in the center. The appearance is ruffled and dense with petals.

Rosette
Smaller, petal-filled flower forms that fan outward from a cupped base.

PETAL COUNTS

Single: Roses with between four and eight petals

Semi-double: Roses with between nine and sixteen petals

Double: Roses with between seventeen and twenty-five petals

Full: Roses with between twenty-six and forty petals

Very Full: Roses with more than forty petals

ROSE FRAGRANCES

Old Rose: The warm, sweet perfume of a traditional rose

Tea: The earthy complexity of fresh tea leaves

Musk: A rich, sweet scent, like cloves

Myrrh: A spicy, warm anise-like scent

Fruity: In a range from a citrusy scent of lemon or grapefruit to notes of a stone fruit, berry, or even hints of banana

TYPES OF ROSES

THE THOUSANDS OF VARIETIES OF ROSES ARE DIVIDED INTO THREE distinct categories: antique (or old garden) roses, species (or wild) roses, and modern roses.

Antique roses include the Gallica, Damask, Alba, and Centifolia varieties, which were cultivated prior to the mid-nineteenth century. Old garden roses are incredibly beautiful and put on quite the show, but after their spring bloom many will not bloom again until the following year—so while the romantic in me loves to collect old garden roses, they're not particularly suited for growing as cut flowers.

Species roses are found in the wild and lack the crossbreeding of modern and antique roses. Wild roses typically have a single five-petal bloom, and they're almost always pink. While these rose types are lovely, they are usually very thorny and do not last long in a vase.

Modern roses are the best option for a cutting garden. Bred after 1867, these roses are hybridized, with the best traits from multiple roses combined to make up each new variety. Most modern roses bloom continuously from spring through fall, have large flower heads, are fragrant, and are disease resistant. They look equally beautiful in the garden and in the vase. Of all the classes of modern roses, following are the six main types we love to grow and share at our farm: hybrid tea, floribunda, grandiflora, shrub, English, and climbing roses. (Note, not included in this roundup, because they are not suitable for cutting, are ground cover roses. These are mostly ornamental, and ideal for a walkway or covering a slope.)

Included in each profile are a list of my favorite varieties; their general growth habit, size, and bloom time; and in which USDA Hardiness Zones they will thrive. (For more on determining your climate zone, turn to page 206.)

· HYBRID TEA ROSES ·

Sweet Mademoiselle

Hybrid teas are one of the most popular types of roses and can be found in every climate. First created by crossing a tea rose with a hybrid perpetual rose, they are stately plants with ornate blooms that are borne on long stems, easy to recognize for their distinctive, upright shape, intense fragrance, and large pointed buds. While their petal count is typically thirty to fifty petals, they grow to be substantial flowers and can make a grand statement.

Hybrid teas have been bred thousands of times, and there are always new varieties coming to market. They can be found in every imaginable color to suit any garden's palette, and over the years hybridizers have even bred varieties that resemble old-fashioned blooms.

I think of hybrid tea roses as the backbone of the rose garden. To mask their rigid structure, we like to place them in the back of the garden bed, where their size can be appreciated.

Hybrid teas have very identifiable flushes, or times when the rose is in full bloom. This means that plants will put on a beautiful show and then have a period of rest while they grow new foliage and buds for the next bloom. In our climate, hybrid tea roses flush approximately every six to eight weeks. Regular deadheading will shorten the time between bloom cycles. For specific tips on deadheading, see page 257.

HARDINESS ZONES: 5 to 10

GROWTH HABIT: Upright bushy habit

SIZE: 3 to 8 feet (0.9 to 2.4 m) tall and 2 to 3 feet (0.6 to 0.9 m) wide

BLOOM TIME: Repeat bloom from late spring to fall

NOTEWORTHY VARIETIES: Francis Meilland (page 69), Apricots n' Cream (page 42), Clouds of Glory (page 163), Sweet Mademoiselle (page 79)

· FLORIBUNDA ROSES ·

Out of Africa

We grow more floribundas than any other type of rose because of how simple they are to maintain and how many blooms they produce. The plants are compact (3 to 4 feet/0.9 to 1.2 m tall and wide) and bloom continuously all season long with very little intervention. Our floribundas are almost never without flowers, and thankfully so, since they're the most popular roses we offer!

First developed around 1940, these hybrid roses combine a free-flowering nature and compact habit with a vibrant color range. Like their larger counterpart, grandifloras (page 22), floribundas bloom in sprays, which consist of a terminal center bloom and three to five side blooms. These blooms tend to be smaller than those of hybrid teas, but because they grow in clusters, just a few stems can fill an entire vase.

I believe floribunda roses are the prettiest plants in the rose garden. They typically have full, lush foliage all the way to the ground, covering the entire plant, and they maintain a bushy, shrub-like appearance. They are lovely in mixed cottage-style borders, planted en masse on a slope for erosion control, as privacy hedging, or in containers. They are ideal for beginners who want to grow roses and don't yet have the time or knowledge to care for higher-maintenance varieties. Floribundas are a rose for every garden and every rose gardener!

HARDINESS ZONES: 4 to 10

GROWTH HABIT: Compact bushy habit

SIZE: 2 to 5 feet (0.6 to 1.5 m) tall and 2 to 4 feet (0.6 to 1.2 m) wide

BLOOM TIME: Repeat bloom from early summer to fall

NOTEWORTHY VARIETIES: Koko Loko (page 130), Distant Drums (page 84), Life of the Party (page 198)

· GRANDIFLORA ROSES ·

All Dressed Up

Grandifloras are bred by crossing a hybrid tea rose (page 20) with a floribunda (page 21) and are the best of both worlds: tall, striking plants with elegant, abundant blooms like the hybrid tea and the continuous blooming cycles of the floribunda. One of my favorite roses, All Dressed Up, is a grandiflora of momentous proportions. If you're looking for a continuously flowering rose and have ample space, I would recommend grandifloras. These rosebushes range in height from variety to variety, but generally speaking, floribundas are better suited for more compact gardens.

Grandifloras make excellent cut flowers because they are packed with blooms. These roses are especially appropriate for large formal gardens where the gardener wants a mix of tall and short bushes for multiple levels of interest.

HARDINESS ZONES: 5 to 10

GROWTH HABIT: Very upright bushy habit

SIZE: Up to 8 feet (2.4 m) tall and 2 to 5 feet (0.6 to 1.5 m) wide

BLOOM TIME: Repeat blooming from spring to first frost

NOTEWORTHY VARIETIES: Stephen Rulo (page 186), Honey Dijon (page 191), Crazy Love (page 33), All Dressed Up (page 56)

· SHRUB ROSES ·

Scentuous

Shrub roses are generous, rounded plants that make wonderful borders and hedges. They can sprawl anywhere from 5 to 15 feet (1.5 to 4.6 m) wide and are bred to be extremely cold hardy. Pure Perfume is a perfect example of an exemplary shrub rose: It lines one of our garden borders, and since we planted the roses 4 feet (1.2 m) from one another, they seem to form a continuous, glorious hedge that's in constant bloom. Along a pathway, shrub roses make a graceful and bold statement.

Shrub roses, while not as showy as other types of roses, are easy to maintain and provide consistent color in the garden. Blooms are produced in bountiful, fragrant clusters that are typically long enough for cutting.

HARDINESS ZONES: 3 to 11

GROWTH HABIT: Mounding, bushy, spreading or ground cover habit

SIZE: 1 to 20 feet (0.3 to 6.1 m) tall and 5 to 15 feet (1.5 to 4.6 m) wide

BLOOM TIME: Varies according to variety. These include one-time bloomers from late spring to early summer, as well as repeat and continuous bloomers that flower from late spring to frost.

NOTEWORTHY VARIETIES: Pure Perfume (page 178), Candice (page 91), Scentuous (page 58)

· ENGLISH ROSES ·

Grace

There are hundreds of English varieties, and I've grown almost all of them. Their rosette and cup-shaped blooms boast up to 150 petals and are filled with a classic tea rose fragrance. These large, arching plants can best be described as romantic—their sight evokes splendor and whimsy. Contemporary English roses offer the gardener a nostalgic look with many of the benefits of modern roses: They have been bred for disease resistance and to be lower maintenance than their beautiful ancestors, old garden roses.

English roses are among the most popular roses with home gardeners because of their country cottage look. We grow David Austin roses, which are hybrids, bred by crossing modern roses with old garden roses. They are typically large shrubs or climbers, and they combine a full-petaled flower form with the intense fragrance of antique roses. They repeatedly bloom throughout the season and have an excellent vase life. English roses are beautiful in a mixed border, in containers, as hedges, grown on arbors and arches, and as stunning focal points in the garden.

HARDINESS ZONES: 4 to 11

GROWTH HABIT: Upright, bushy, or climbing habit

SIZE: 4 to 12 feet (1.2 to 3.7 m) tall and 3 to 5 feet (0.9 to 1.5 m) wide

BLOOM TIME: Repeat or continuous bloom from late spring until fall

NOTEWORTHY VARIETIES: Emily Brontë (page 87), Carding Mill (page 38), The Lady Gardener (page 94)

· CLIMBING ROSES ·

Eden

There are few things more enchanting in the spring than roses covering an arbor, arch, or garden shed. To walk through an arch awash with roses is an experience even people who don't love roses will enjoy. When climbing roses are allowed to grow to their maximum size, whether they're trained to attach to a structure or pegged (page 235), they are festooned with blooms that make their canes gracefully arch over and touch the ground.

Roses that climb are charming, whimsical, and easy to grow. There is a wild, untamed manner about them and they're considerably less fussy than their shrub counterparts. They can be kept as tidy as one prefers or left to grow freely. Simple, routine maintenance to mildly train their canes will give them structure.

Climbing roses come in every color imaginable. They are ideal for covering anything unsightly, creating a privacy border, or just enjoying in the garden where they will have the space to grow.

HARDINESS ZONES: 4 to 11

GROWTH HABIT: Long, vining, climbing habit

SIZE: 6 to 12 feet (1.8 to 3.7 m) tall and 3 to 4 feet (0.9 to 1.2 m) wide

BLOOM TIME: Varies according to variety. This type includes one-time bloomers from late spring to early summer as well as repeat and continuous bloomers that flower from late spring to frost.

NOTEWORTHY VARIETIES: Eden (page 73), New Dawn (page 113), Sombreuil (page 176)

CHAPTER TWO

The BEST VARIETIES for CUTTING and ARRANGING

There is a rose for just about every mood, fragrance, color, and look you could imagine. While there are hundreds of gorgeous varieties to choose from, not all of them make good cut roses. The pages that follow highlight my favorite rose varieties, sorted by color, that meet high standards for cutability, health, hardiness, and, of course, beauty. From showstopping hybrid teas with bold colors to wispy, neutral English shrub roses, the array of roses featured here ensures you'll find something to match your garden style.

APRICOT
and
PEACH

THIS FLORIBUNDA NEVER STOPS
blooming, with rich clusters of 4-inch (10 cm)
ruffled flowers in a brilliant array of hues.
In our climate, these roses can turn a deep
pumpkin orange in the hottest part of the year,
transitioning to a peach to apricot tipped with
pink when milder weather arrives. I much
prefer Soul Sister when our weather cools
down, and I think this rose also appreciates a
reprieve from heat—its blooms are massive in
milder conditions.

With a sweet fragrance, Soul Sister is
a pretty addition to any garden and a rose
that's very simple to care for. Where we live in
Southern California, powdery mildew can form
on its buds and foliage; however, that shouldn't
deter gardeners from enjoying this rose. For
tips on spotting and treating powdery mildew,
see page 247.

One of the most notable things about Soul
Sister is its staying power. Not only does this
rose bloom all season long, but the flowers on
the plants will last more than a week before
wilting. And its ruffled petals really make
this rose stand out in the apricot and peach
category. It's bright and cheerful and will
provide enough cut flowers to gift your friends
and neighbors.

BASICS

ROSE TYPE:	Floribunda
BREEDER:	Kordes
COLOR:	Peach to apricot
FRAGRANCE:	Mild
BLOOM FORM:	Cupped
PETAL COUNT:	26 to 40
GROWTH TYPE:	Short shrub
BLOOM TIME:	Blooms continuously

PLANTING

PLANTING SEASON:	Spring
LIGHT REQUIREMENTS:	Full sun
HARDINESS ZONES:	5 to 10
SPACING:	4 feet (1.2 m)
HEIGHT:	3 feet (0.9 m)
WIDTH:	3 feet (0.9 m)
DISEASE RESISTANCE:	Very good
CONTAINER PLANTING:	No

ANTICO AMORE IS AN ITALIAN ROSE
that combines form and function. Bred by Barni
in 1988, this romantic hybrid tea variety is as
disease resistant as it is lovely. I've always been
drawn to roses that aren't one solid color, and
Antico Amore boasts a natural gradient with a
deep peachy heart that gives way to light and
translucent outer petals as the rose ages.

The dense blooms of Antico Amore feature
many petals and will open to be 4 to 5 inches
(10 to 13 cm) wide. Though the blooms are
substantial, the plant itself does not grow to
be too large, making it suitable for any garden.
This variety is easy to grow and will perform
well in Zones 6 to 10, though warmer climates
will see blooms in a pinker rather than peach
tone. Its light, sweet, and fruity perfume is a
treat to enjoy during this rose's long vase life.
If your heart is set on a romantic, old-world
rose that is easy to care for and harvest, Antico
Amore is a wonderful choice.

BASICS

ROSE TYPE:	Hybrid tea
BREEDER:	Barni
COLOR:	Peach
FRAGRANCE:	Mild
BLOOM FORM:	Cupped
PETAL COUNT:	20 to 40
GROWTH TYPE:	Medium upright shrub
BLOOM TIME:	Repeat spring through fall

PLANTING

PLANTING SEASON:	Spring
LIGHT REQUIREMENTS:	Full sun
HARDINESS ZONES:	6 to 10
SPACING:	3 to 4 feet (0.9 to 1.2 m)
HEIGHT:	3 to 4 feet (0.9 to 1.2 m)
WIDTH:	2 to 3 feet (0.6 to 0.9 m)
DISEASE RESISTANCE:	Excellent
CONTAINER PLANTING:	No

· CRAZY LOVE ·

PART OF THE SUNBELT LINE OF ROSES BY Kordes, Crazy Love is bred in Germany and is a good choice for gardeners who live in colder and very warm climates alike.

Hardiness aside, the most notable aspect of this grandiflora rose is its magnificent shading. The buds of Crazy Love start out in orangey sunset tones. As the bud opens and ages, it gives way to an intense coppery center that unfolds into ruffles of fading blush tones, culminating in opalescent outer petals for a shimmering ombré effect.

This rose is a healthy, disease-resistant plant that blooms reliably all year long. Grandifloras can typically grow to be very large, but Crazy Love will only reach a moderate width, about 4 feet (1.2 m) square. It would be a striking option for any landscape.

BASICS

ROSE TYPE:	Grandiflora
BREEDER:	Kordes
COLOR:	Yellow, copper, pink
FRAGRANCE:	Mild
BLOOM FORM:	Rosette
PETAL COUNT:	100-plus
GROWTH TYPE:	Upright and bushy
BLOOM TIME:	Repeat

PLANTING

PLANTING SEASON:	Spring
LIGHT REQUIREMENTS:	Full sun
HARDINESS ZONES:	5 to 10
SPACING:	4 feet (1.2 m)
HEIGHT:	3 to 4 feet (0.9 to 1.2 m)
WIDTH:	3.5 feet (1.1 m)
DISEASE RESISTANCE:	Very good
CONTAINER PLANTING:	No

NAMED AFTER THE BELOVED BRITISH children's book author, Roald Dahl is an English shrub rose bred by David Austin. The plant bears medium-sized cupped rosettes with sunset orange to apricot to ochre tones that cascade across the petals, creating a memorable, jovial hue. Though this rose isn't prominent like a hybrid tea—its full blooms measure about 2.5 inches (6 cm)—its golden sprays will send a cheerful welcome to all who pass its sweet rosettes.

Roald Dahl flowers very reliably and abundantly, needs very little intervention, and is disease resistant. While some shrubs can be trained to climb, this variety minds its manners in the garden, so it's ideal for container gardeners or accompanying other rose varieties. Roald Dahl is also a variety with hardly any thorns, so it is a safe choice for gardeners with children or pets.

At my previous farm we had Roald Dahl planted every 2 feet (0.6 m) along either side of our driveway, forming a beautiful, flowing hedge as we drove up. The golden blooms and delightful fragrance of these roses gave us a warm, happy feeling—one I remember fondly to this day.

BASICS

ROSE TYPE:	English shrub
BREEDER:	David Austin
COLOR:	Apricot to golden
FRAGRANCE:	Mild
BLOOM FORM:	Cupped
PETAL COUNT:	55
GROWTH TYPE:	Shrub
BLOOM TIME:	Spring through fall

PLANTING

PLANTING SEASON:	Spring
LIGHT REQUIREMENTS:	Full sun
HARDINESS ZONES:	5 to 10
SPACING:	3 feet (0.9 m)
HEIGHT:	4 feet (1.2 m)
WIDTH:	4 feet (1.2 m)
DISEASE RESISTANCE:	Excellent
CONTAINER PLANTING:	Yes

RARELY DO I SAY A ROSE IS PERFECT, but Bathsheba is an exception. I was immediately enamored with David Austin's recent introduction when it was first announced in the UK. I had to wait an additional year for Bathsheba to arrive in the US, and to say I was full of anticipation would be an understatement. Peach roses aren't always a favorite of mine, but there is something so sweet and innocent about this English beauty.

Bathsheba was named after the heroine of Thomas Hardy's novel *Far from the Madding Crowd* and features blooms that open to shallow cups. The many-petaled double rosettes are borne on stems that contain multiple buds. Bathsheba's beautiful blend of subtle apricot-pink and soft yellow flowers gives an overall impression of apricot blooms with creamy, washed-out outer petals. There is a deep floral and myrrh fragrance with notes of honey and tea.

One of the loveliest aspects of Bathsheba is that it is a short, mannerly climbing rose. Its vigor is excellent, and it is easily kept at a size that all gardeners can manage. There are some climbers, especially English roses, that require a great deal of space, but Bathsheba can be enjoyed in small and large gardens alike. At our farm, we weave the tender canes on iron obelisks. Bathsheba will provide a succession of exquisite, petal-packed rosettes, even as a younger rose in the garden (less than two years old).

BASICS

ROSE TYPE:	English shrub
BREEDER:	David Austin
COLOR:	Apricot-yellow
FRAGRANCE:	Medium
BLOOM FORM:	Cupped rosettes
PETAL COUNT:	170-plus
GROWTH TYPE:	Climbing
BLOOM TIME:	Repeat

PLANTING

PLANTING SEASON:	Spring
LIGHT REQUIREMENTS:	Full sun
HARDINESS ZONES:	5 to 10
SPACING:	4 to 5 feet (1.2 to 1.5 m)
HEIGHT:	8 to 10 feet (2.4 to 3 m)
WIDTH:	2 to 3 feet (0.6 to 0.9 m)
DISEASE RESISTANCE:	Very good
CONTAINER PLANTING:	No

CARDING MILL IS A FAN FAVORITE, which is why we have more than five hundred of these plants growing at our farm. Named after Carding Mill Valley in England's beautiful Long Mynd, this is one of David Austin's perfect apricot roses. Carding Mill keeps its true apricot color throughout the changing of seasons, whereas other varieties will drift toward pink or peach in different temperatures.

Many of David Austin's roses are massive and, as such, aren't good choices for container gardening or balcony plantings. Carding Mill is the exception, reaching only 3 to 4 feet (0.9 to 1.2 m), even in our warm climate and with vigorous cutting. It also happens to be a great variety for beginner rose gardeners; just stick it in the ground, give it a bit of fertilizer in the spring, and off it will go!

The buds appear coral-reddish in color, but as the petals begin to open, the true apricot tone reveals itself. Carding Mill reminds me of a water lily, with flat, slightly pointy petals fanned out along the bottom of the bloom, which unfolds elegantly. The cheerful apricot blooms and bright green foliage work beautifully in spring arrangements, but the rose also boasts an unexpected spicy myrrh scent with hints of pumpkin, which gives it a very autumnal feel.

Carding Mill is a great cut flower, but once it begins to open, it tends to proceed quickly. Therefore, we cut this rose when the sepals have just come down from the bud. If you cut it when the bloom is fully open, by the time you get it in water, it will barely last a day in a vase.

BASICS

ROSE TYPE:	English shrub
BREEDER:	David Austin
COLOR:	Apricot
FRAGRANCE:	Medium
BLOOM FORM:	Rosette
PETAL COUNT:	80
GROWTH TYPE:	Bushy shrub
BLOOM TIME:	Repeat

PLANTING

PLANTING SEASON:	Spring
LIGHT REQUIREMENTS:	Full sun / partial shade
HARDINESS ZONES:	5 to 10
SPACING:	4 feet (1.2 m)
HEIGHT:	4 feet (1.2 m)
WIDTH:	3.5 feet (1.1 m)
DISEASE RESISTANCE:	Excellent
CONTAINER PLANTING:	Yes

IT'S NOT VERY OFTEN THAT I'M STOPPED in my tracks by a hybrid tea rose, but Marilyn Monroe proves to be an exception time and again. This peach perfection, befitting the legendary actress, is utterly feminine. It boasts graceful, foliage-filled stems, and its creamy apricot buds open to buxom 5- to 6-inch (13 to 15 cm) blooms. I have never seen another peach rose with such thick, long-lasting petals, making this an ideal cut flower.

Marilyn Monroe is a valuable addition to our collection of peach roses for its lasting beauty. This rose flowers profusely in all weather and never fades. When all the other roses have dropped their petals, Marilyn can be found fully adorned with blooms.

BASICS

ROSE TYPE:	Hybrid tea
BREEDER:	Tom Carruth
COLOR:	Pale peach
FRAGRANCE:	Mild
BLOOM FORM:	Cupped
PETAL COUNT:	17 to 25
GROWTH TYPE:	Upright
BLOOM TIME:	Repeat

PLANTING

PLANTING SEASON:	Spring
LIGHT REQUIREMENTS:	Full sun
HARDINESS ZONES:	6 to 10
SPACING:	4 feet (1.2 m)
HEIGHT:	3 to 4 feet (0.9 to 1.2 m)
WIDTH:	4 feet (1.2 m)
DISEASE RESISTANCE:	Excellent
CONTAINER PLANTING:	No

ONE OF THE REASONS WE DECIDED TO grow State of Grace is because of our extensive and enjoyable experience growing its relative Distant Drums (page 84). Sharing the vigor and repetitive bloom cycle of Distant Drums, State of Grace is equally beautiful. This rose grows long, soft canes from the base of the plant and has a graceful, arching, shrub-like appearance.

The blooms of this variety are borne in clusters on long, thorny stems. If you're not a fan of thorns, State of Grace may not be for you. However, I think it's worth a spot in the garden due to its stunningly diverse color: Its buds are a saturated red that open to a dusty peach, and the reverse of its petals are a deep orange. And it only becomes lovelier as its flowers age. Each stem has up to four blooms, so just a handful will give you a large bouquet.

BASICS

ROSE TYPE:	Grandiflora
BREEDER:	Christian Bédard
COLOR:	Golden-yellow, apricot, pink
FRAGRANCE:	Medium
BLOOM FORM:	Old-fashioned
PETAL COUNT:	40-plus
GROWTH TYPE:	Medium bushy
BLOOM TIME:	Repeat

PLANTING

PLANTING SEASON:	Spring
LIGHT REQUIREMENTS:	Full sun
HARDINESS ZONES:	6 to 10
SPACING:	4 feet (1.2 m)
HEIGHT:	3 to 4 feet (0.9 to 1.2 m)
WIDTH:	4 feet (1.2 m)
DISEASE RESISTANCE:	Excellent
CONTAINER PLANTING:	No

· APRICOTS N' CREAM ·

ONE OF OUR NEWEST ADDITIONS TO THE farm, this gorgeous Romantica rose from the French breeder Meilland entered the US market in 2012 but had limited availability until recently. Now that Apricots n' Cream has joined our collection, I wonder how I ever lived without it. Its cup-shaped cabbage blooms are thick with petals and range in color from apricot to peach to blush, even on a single plant. Sometimes I'll come across a bloom that is a deep apricot in the center and fades out to blush, an effect that gives this variety its name. On the same plant I'll spot a pure peach bloom. Some growers prize uniformity, but I love the variations this rose displays.

Apricots n' Cream has quickly become a customer favorite because of its romantic palette and shape and beautiful quartered blooms. Its fragrance is that of a typical tea rose, with a hint of sweetness.

An upright plant, Apricots n' Cream blooms in prolific clusters. The blooms are very round, with a high petal count, which means in moist or coastal climates with high humidity this rose will be susceptible to botrytis blight (see page 246). It's best suited for dry climates, so our farm in Zone 10 provides ideal conditions for this vigorous bloomer.

BASICS

ROSE TYPE:	Hybrid tea
BREEDER:	Meilland
COLOR:	Apricot
FRAGRANCE:	Mild
BLOOM FORM:	Cupped, old-fashioned, cabbage
PETAL COUNT:	40-plus
GROWTH TYPE:	Bushy shrub
BLOOM TIME:	Repeat

PLANTING

PLANTING SEASON:	Spring
LIGHT REQUIREMENTS:	Full sun
HARDINESS ZONES:	5 to 10
SPACING:	4 feet (1.2 m)
HEIGHT:	5 feet (1.5 m)
WIDTH:	3 feet (0.9 m)
DISEASE RESISTANCE:	Excellent
CONTAINER PLANTING:	No

• CROWN PRINCESS MARGARETA •

CROWN PRINCESS MARGARETA, A granddaughter of Queen Victoria, was known for creating the beautiful gardens at her Summer Palace—Sofiero Castle in Helsingborg, Sweden—alongside her husband, King Gustavus VI Adolfus. David Austin thought it fitting to name this glorious garden rose after this skilled Swedish gardener.

I first began growing Crown Princess Margareta in 2015 and was immediately drawn to its deep cup-shaped, scalloped blooms. In our warm western climate, the flowers are a dusty, pale peach with the slightest blush hue. In cooler climates, Crown Princess Margareta is a much brighter peach-to-apricot color. Its scent is strong tea rose layered with fruit. I once clipped the most heavenly bloom of Crown Princess Margareta and carried it around all day to take in the scent.

I like to call this a sprawling rose. It bears long, arching canes that grow outward more than upward (like a hybrid tea would), so it requires space if it's allowed to grow freely—though it can also be trained to grow on an arch. This rose is equally impressive both ways and while the blooms aren't the longest lasting, they are worthy of cutting and enjoying in the vase.

BASICS

ROSE TYPE:	English shrub
BREEDER:	David Austin
COLOR:	Apricot-orange
FRAGRANCE:	Strong
BLOOM FORM:	Cupped
PETAL COUNT:	120
GROWTH TYPE:	Arching shrub or medium climber
BLOOM TIME:	Repeat

PLANTING

PLANTING SEASON:	Spring
LIGHT REQUIREMENTS:	Full sun
HARDINESS ZONES:	4 to 8
SPACING:	4 to 5 feet (1.2 to 1.5 m)
HEIGHT:	12 feet (3.7 m) as a climber
WIDTH:	4 feet (1.2 m)
DISEASE RESISTANCE:	Excellent
CONTAINER PLANTING:	No

• POLKA •

I VIVIDLY REMEMBER THE FIRST TIME I saw this rose. While attending a wedding, I noticed a breathtaking arch covered in roses, leading to the aisle where the bride would make her debut. At first glance I thought the roses on this marvelous plant were fake because I had never seen blooms so enormous and plentiful before. Seeing is believing with Polka, and you must experience this rose in person to truly appreciate how impressive it is.

This climbing rose has an old-rose look, with the modern benefits of repeat flowering, winter hardiness, and disease tolerance. Because Polka grows well in both warm and cold climates, it belongs in every rose lover's garden—if space permits. Polka will take as much room as you give it and can grow arching canes that will cover trellises, sheds, or anything else you provide as support.

This apricot rose is known for its massive 6-inch (15 cm) blooms—each so stunning that a single one in a vase will make a resounding impact. During the warmest months, Polka's striking apricot hue will turn to more of a peachy shade. I prefer the more subdued, less saturated version of this rose, as it reminds me of gently washed textiles that get better over time. Polka's warm fragrance will fill a room with a lovely spice and pepper scent.

BASICS

ROSE TYPE:	Climbing
BREEDER:	Jacques Mouchotte, Meilland
COLOR:	Peach
FRAGRANCE:	Very strong
BLOOM FORM:	Old-fashioned
PETAL COUNT:	17 to 25
GROWTH TYPE:	Climbing
BLOOM TIME:	Repeat

PLANTING

PLANTING SEASON:	Spring
LIGHT REQUIREMENTS:	Full sun
HARDINESS ZONES:	5 to 10
SPACING:	5 feet (1.5 m)
HEIGHT:	8 to 12 feet (2.4 to 3.7 m)
WIDTH:	4 feet (1.2 m)
DISEASE RESISTANCE:	Very good
CONTAINER PLANTING:	No

PINK

JUBILEE CELEBRATION, NAMED TO commemorate Queen Elizabeth II's Golden Jubilee, is an amazing shrub rose that, when planted in multiples, looks like a thick blanket of stunning coral-pink. When showing friends around our farm, I make a point of bringing them by a Jubilee Celebration rose just to show off its amazing scent, which is heavy with citrus and fruit.

This hardy plant makes for a wonderful cut rose. Its stems can be long, often with clusters of graceful, nodding blooms. The petals are coral-pink, changing to a light salmon during the heat of summer. When the stem is cut as the sepals are down, the vase life of Jubilee Celebration is exceptionally long: five to seven days. Just a few stems in a vase will fill your home with a sweet, intoxicating fragrance for days.

BASICS

ROSE TYPE:	English shrub
BREEDER:	David Austin
COLOR:	Coral-pink
FRAGRANCE:	Strong
BLOOM FORM:	Cupped
PETAL COUNT:	90
GROWTH TYPE:	Shrub
BLOOM TIME:	Repeat

PLANTING

PLANTING SEASON:	Spring
LIGHT REQUIREMENTS:	Full sun
HARDINESS ZONES:	6 to 10
SPACING:	4 feet (1.2 m)
HEIGHT:	4 feet (1.2 m)
WIDTH:	4 feet (1.2 m)
DISEASE RESISTANCE:	Good
CONTAINER PLANTING:	Yes

A WELL-BRED, HEALTHY GERMAN ROSE from Kordes, Bliss Parfuma is extraordinary. It is softly scented with double blooms that can measure up to 6 inches (15 cm) across, which is impressive considering they're borne on such a compact plant. The stems of this variety are also long and well positioned to harvest.

This blush to peach rose performs well in both heat and humidity and will repeat quickly with deadheading. When it is used in an arrangement, your eye is drawn to Bliss Parfuma immediately and all the other flowers fade away. I wish I had begun growing this rose earlier, as it has become such a favorite of mine. For those seeking a very manageable rosebush in enchanting feminine tones, Bliss Parfuma would be a lovely addition to your garden.

BASICS

ROSE TYPE:	Floribunda
BREEDER:	Kordes
COLOR:	Blush to peach
FRAGRANCE:	Mild
BLOOM FORM:	Cupped
PETAL COUNT:	41-plus
GROWTH TYPE:	Short shrub
BLOOM TIME:	Repeat

PLANTING

PLANTING SEASON:	Spring
LIGHT REQUIREMENTS:	Full sun
HARDINESS ZONES:	4 to 10
SPACING:	3 to 4 feet (0.9 to 1.2 m)
HEIGHT:	3 feet (0.9 m)
WIDTH:	3 feet (0.9 m)
DISEASE RESISTANCE:	Excellent
CONTAINER PLANTING:	No

GENTLE HERMIONE IS A SWEET AND dazzling English rose with a deep myrrh and old-rose scent. Displaying nostalgic old-world character, Gentle Hermione is the perfect choice for those wanting a delicate, pale pink rose in their garden. This variety's shallow-cupped blooms open fully to reveal golden stamens that fade as they mature. The flowers are perfectly formed, making them ideal for cutting and arranging in the vase.

In the garden, Gentle Hermione is a stunning shrub that minds its manners by growing quickly but not so much that it takes space from other roses. We grow Gentle Hermione in the front of the rose bed, surrounded by herbs. The plant has gently arching stems and the blooms are especially tolerant of rain, making it a wonderful rose for wet climates. Charming and timeless Gentle Hermione will always have a place in my garden.

BASICS

ROSE TYPE:	English shrub
BREEDER:	David Austin
COLOR:	Pale blush
FRAGRANCE:	Strong
BLOOM FORM:	Cupped
PETAL COUNT:	90
GROWTH TYPE:	Shrub
BLOOM TIME:	Repeat

PLANTING

PLANTING SEASON:	Spring
LIGHT REQUIREMENTS:	Full sun
HARDINESS ZONES:	4 to 9
SPACING:	4 feet (1.2 m)
HEIGHT:	4 feet (1.2 m)
WIDTH:	3 feet (0.9 m)
DISEASE RESISTANCE:	Excellent
CONTAINER PLANTING:	No

· AUGUSTA LUISE ·

BORNE ON A SINGLE STEM, EACH FLOWER on Augusta Luise is a feast for the eyes. This hybrid tea features delightfully large pompon blooms. The ruffled petals open like an aging sunset, producing a peachy center with spectacular salmon-pink outer petals. The fragrance has high fruity notes, and its hardiness and majestic color make it a highly coveted variety among both gardeners and floral designers.

While the blooms of Augusta Luise are massive in comparison with other varieties—over 6 inches (15 cm) in diameter—the plant itself is mannerly and will only grow to about 3 to 4 feet (0.9 to 1.2 m) wide. Augusta Luise makes a perfect garden rose and cut flower. It's not the most productive, but it is well worth the wait as the color and fragrance of this rose when it finally blooms are so fantastic and memorable.

The hues of the flowers will differ in various climates and will age beautifully as it opens. The single-stem structure of Augusta Luise makes it easy to cut, and it enjoys a vase life of seven to nine days.

BASICS

ROSE TYPE:	Hybrid tea
BREEDER:	Tantau
COLOR:	Pink to peach
FRAGRANCE:	Strong
BLOOM FORM:	Old-fashioned
PETAL COUNT:	50
GROWTH TYPE:	Bushy, upright
BLOOM TIME:	Repeat

PLANTING

PLANTING SEASON:	Spring
LIGHT REQUIREMENTS:	Full sun
HARDINESS ZONES:	6 to 10
SPACING:	4 feet (1.2 m)
HEIGHT:	4 to 5 feet (1.2 to 1.5 m)
WIDTH:	3 to 4 feet (0.9 to 1.2 m)
DISEASE RESISTANCE:	Excellent
CONTAINER PLANTING:	No

WHEN WEEKS ROSES REACHED OUT A
few years ago and asked if I wanted to trial All
Dressed Up—a bountiful, full-bodied rose bred
by Christian Bédard—I jumped at the chance.

Old-fashioned in form with cup-shaped
blooms and luscious pink petals, this rose
resembles an antique or English rose, but
because of its newer breeding status, it behaves
in a decidedly modern way. It repeats its bloom
cycles quickly and is disease-free, making it
an easy and lovely addition to any garden.
The coloring is a cheerful, lively shade of pink,
accompanied by rich green foliage. All Dressed
Up blooms in massive sprays, usually with one
huge center bloom and generous side stems that
are cuttable themselves and work perfectly in
bud vases.

This hardy rose was bred to have a long
vase life of ten to fourteen days, but the trade-
off is its lack of intense fragrance. I like to pair
All Dressed Up with a more fragrant rose in
the same vase. If you find the fragrant roses
drooping after a few days, switch them out with
new roses for the duration of All Dressed Up's
vase life.

BASICS

ROSE TYPE:	Grandiflora
BREEDER:	Christian Bédard
COLOR:	Pink
FRAGRANCE:	Medium
BLOOM FORM:	Quartered, cupped
PETAL COUNT:	40-plus
GROWTH TYPE:	Upright
BLOOM TIME:	Repeat

PLANTING

PLANTING SEASON:	Spring
LIGHT REQUIREMENTS:	Full sun, partial shade
HARDINESS ZONES:	5 to 9
SPACING:	4 feet (1.2 m)
HEIGHT:	5 to 6 feet (1.5 to 1.8 m)
WIDTH:	4 feet (1.2 m)
DISEASE RESISTANCE:	Excellent
CONTAINER PLANTING:	No

SCENTUOUS IS A GERMAN ROSE, BRED BY
Hans Jürgen Evers for Tantau, with English-
style cottage garden rose features. As its name
suggests, it has a rich, intoxicating fragrance:
a honey tea rose scent with an end note of pure
sweetness. It's a smell so delectable you'll find
your face deep in these blooms!

Aside from the symphony of fragrance, I
love the ruffled and swirled cabbage centers of
Scentuous's blossoms. The petals fade out to
an almost clear ballet pink to nearly white on
the outer petals. The near-perfect flowers are
borne on clusters, bringing even more joyous
fragrance and beauty to the garden and the
vase.

Ideal for planting in Zones 5 to 10, Scentuous
will grow to about 4 to 5 feet (1.2 to 1.5 m) in
height, forming a bushy, prominent shrub. Herbs
and companion plants will help this rose sing,
adding more charm to this rose's cottage vibe.
(For more on companion planting, see page 217.)

BASICS

ROSE TYPE:	Shrub rose
BREEDER:	Hans Jürgen Evers
COLOR:	Light pink
FRAGRANCE:	Strong
BLOOM FORM:	Cupped
PETAL COUNT:	40-plus
GROWTH TYPE:	Bushy
BLOOM TIME:	Repeat

PLANTING

PLANTING SEASON:	Spring
LIGHT REQUIREMENTS:	Full sun
HARDINESS ZONES:	5 to 10
SPACING:	4 feet (1.2 m)
HEIGHT:	4 to 5 feet (1.2 to 1.5 m)
WIDTH:	4 feet (1.2 m)
DISEASE RESISTANCE:	Excellent
CONTAINER PLANTING:	No

· CHICAGO PEACE ·

CHICAGO PEACE IS THE CHILD OF THE
Peace rose (page 185)—one of the most famous
and celebrated varieties in the world. No two
blooms are the same on this plant. Chicago
Peace's flowers run the gamut of the peach-
to-pink-to-yellow color spectrum, rolling
across the petals from creamy yellow centers
to shocking pink and peach tones with orange
undertones. From one watercolored petal to the
next, the hues on Chicago Peace's blooms leave
a lasting, sorbet-colored impact.

   When I first started growing roses, I had
twenty Chicago Peace plants lining one of my
outdoor staircases. And when I think back to
the roses that imprinted on me in those early
days of growing, Chicago Peace is the one that
lasts in my memory.

   Just as the color and shading on this variety
is impactful, so too is the fruity, lively, jubilant
fragrance. This is a rose you smell and think to
yourself, "How is that scent possible?" It is that
lovely.

BASICS

ROSE TYPE:	Hybrid tea
BREEDER:	S. Johnston
COLOR:	Pink and yellow
FRAGRANCE:	Moderate
BLOOM FORM:	High-centered
PETAL COUNT:	45
GROWTH TYPE:	Bushy, upright
BLOOM TIME:	Repeat

PLANTING

PLANTING SEASON:	Spring
LIGHT REQUIREMENTS:	Full sun
HARDINESS ZONES:	5 to 10
SPACING:	4 feet (1.2 m)
HEIGHT:	4 to 7 feet (1.2 to 2.1 m)
WIDTH:	3 to 4 feet (0.9 to 1.2 m)
DISEASE RESISTANCE:	Good
CONTAINER PLANTING:	No

· PRINCESS CHARLENE DE MONACO ·

PRINCESS CHARLENE DE MONACO IS ONE of those roses that has it all—large ruffled petals, intoxicatingly sweet fragrance, an abundance of repeating blooms, and long, straight stems—making for a perfect cut flower with an extended vase life. As soon as we added this variety to our garden, we knew we'd need many, many more. Princess Charlene de Monaco quickly became a favorite of ours and is regularly in demand from our customers.

This hybrid tea rose majestically towers over the others in our production fields. By midseason these plants stand close to 7 feet (2.1 m) tall, even after providing us with many beautiful cut stems. The matte green, clean foliage is disease resistant and the soft peach to light pink petals create deep cup-shaped blooms. Because of Princess Charlene de Monaco's grandeur, it's best to plant this upright rose as a focal point or anywhere it won't get in the way of other plants, such as the side or back of your garden.

We experience a range of difficult weather conditions on our farm, despite being in a reliably good rose-growing climate. During one particularly extreme windstorm, we watched in panic as our Princess Charlene de Monaco plants flailed around, bending and rocking in the wind. We were certain the canes would snap and the petals would be damaged beyond repair. However, through it all, these roses remained strong, and the sturdy canes never gave way. This has remained one of our most reliable and hardy roses.

BASICS

ROSE TYPE:	Hybrid tea
BREEDER:	Meilland
COLOR:	Soft pink to peach
FRAGRANCE:	Strong
BLOOM FORM:	Cupped, old-fashioned
PETAL COUNT:	68
GROWTH TYPE:	Upright
BLOOM TIME:	Repeat

PLANTING

PLANTING SEASON:	Spring
LIGHT REQUIREMENTS:	Full sun
HARDINESS ZONES:	5 to 10
SPACING:	4 feet (1.2 m)
HEIGHT:	7 feet (2.1 m)
WIDTH:	4 feet (1.2 m)
DISEASE RESISTANCE:	Excellent
CONTAINER PLANTING:	No

THIS EXQUISITE PINK SHRUB ROSE FROM David Austin is a newer breed, accessible to gardeners in many different climates. Silas Marner has a romantic, flowy look; its relaxed cupped blooms open generously into an array of ruffled, wavy petals. The petals fade out from a lemony heart to varying shades of pearlescent pink, lending the rose a creamy, ethereal quality. This shade progression across the petals makes Silas Marner a perfect rose for companion planting, as its ombré color will add depth and dimension to the garden.

This variety is easy to grow and very prolific, growing from a center terminal flower with side shoots in clusters. Though it is packed with flowers, the shrub itself is mannerly and will stay about 4 by 4 feet (1.2 by 1.2 m). Planting Silas Marner en masse in borders or along pathways will create an overflowing, abundant look in the garden.

Silas Marner has notable burgundy-red foliage (before it turns to green) and a heavenly, unparalleled scent: The fragrance is a citrusy, springy, crisp apple scent with bright notes, which pairs beautifully with its bloom form and color.

BASICS

ROSE TYPE:	English shrub
BREEDER:	David Austin
COLOR:	Light pink
FRAGRANCE:	Medium
BLOOM FORM:	Cupped
PETAL COUNT:	100
GROWTH TYPE:	Bushy
BLOOM TIME:	Repeat

PLANTING

PLANTING SEASON:	Spring
LIGHT REQUIREMENTS:	Full sun
HARDINESS ZONES:	5 to 10
SPACING:	4 feet (1.2 m)
HEIGHT:	3.5 feet (1.1 m)
WIDTH:	4 feet (1.2 m)
DISEASE RESISTANCE:	Excellent
CONTAINER PLANTING:	No

· DESDEMONA ·

DESDEMONA IS A TENDER, WHIMSICAL rose with a fragrance reminiscent of almond blossom and citrus. Named after the tragic heroine of Shakespeare's *Othello*, Desdemona is not a scene-stealer but rather an ideal accent rose. This perfectly sweet variety would be right at home in a charming cottage garden.

Delicate, peachy buds open to beautiful chalice-shaped blooms with around fifty petals each. The fleeting, whimsical beauty of this rose is what makes it so special. Desdemona starts out as a pale, ballet-slipper blush, and as it matures and opens, it fully turns a pearlescent white with a stunning, almost translucent quality. I've never seen another rose with this unique coloring.

In the garden, Desdemona forms a neat, rounded shrub; we have hedges of Desdemona all over our farm. It's a great repeat bloomer, practically always in bud or bloom from early in the spring consistently on through to the first frost. I find that Desdemona pairs beautifully with herbs when landscaping.

The plants are extremely vigorous and grow very quickly. We purchased bare roots of this rose in the spring of 2017 and by that summer they were full-sized (4 by 4 feet/1.2 by 1.2 m) and loaded with buds. Every stem is a spray featuring a center bloom and eight to twelve buds on the side. You can let the center bloom and leave the side buds closed or cut it out and let the sprays fully flower. If the rose is cut when the stems are blooming in sprays, you can have as few as three stems in a vase, yet a full bouquet with over thirty flowers! From fragrance to form, color to bloom shape, everything about Desdemona speaks to its beauty as a soft, whimsical rose.

BASICS

ROSE TYPE:	English shrub
BREEDER:	David Austin
COLOR:	Light blush to white
FRAGRANCE:	Strong
BLOOM FORM:	Cupped
PETAL COUNT:	50-plus
GROWTH TYPE:	Shrub
BLOOM TIME:	Repeat

PLANTING

PLANTING SEASON:	Spring
LIGHT REQUIREMENTS:	Full sun
HARDINESS ZONES:	5 to 9
SPACING:	4 feet (1.2 m)
HEIGHT:	4 feet (1.2 m)
WIDTH:	3 feet (0.9 m)
DISEASE RESISTANCE:	Excellent
CONTAINER PLANTING:	No

QUEEN OF ELEGANCE IS BRED BY ONE OF our friends, Christian Bédard of Weeks Roses. Its parentage lends this rose its unique mauve coloring with pink and purple tones throughout. I've never seen another rose with coloring like Queen of Elegance.

This variety has a spectacular fragrance—deep and spicy, not too roselike. Its stunning, large-headed blooms are borne in clusters, giving them a slight nod. The coloring combined with its fragrance and graceful bowing give this rose a spirit that is romance through and through.

BASICS

ROSE TYPE:	Floribunda
BREEDER:	Christian Bédard
COLOR:	Medium pink to mauve
FRAGRANCE:	Strong
BLOOM FORM:	Old-fashioned
PETAL COUNT:	90
GROWTH TYPE:	Bushy, upright
BLOOM TIME:	Repeat

PLANTING

PLANTING SEASON:	Spring
LIGHT REQUIREMENTS:	Full sun
HARDINESS ZONES:	5 to 10
SPACING:	4 feet (1.2 m)
HEIGHT:	3 to 4 feet (0.9 to 1.2 m)
WIDTH:	2 to 3 feet (0.6 to 0.9 m)
DISEASE RESISTANCE:	Excellent
CONTAINER PLANTING:	No

THIS ENGLISH SHRUB ROSE BY DAVID
Austin grows in the "English garden" in the
front yard of my home, and it makes quite the
impression. The adorable cup-shaped clusters of
The Mill on the Floss feature pale pink blooms
that look as if they've been kissed on the tips of
their petals with a watercolor brush dipped in
deep pink paint. These lively flowers are just
2 to 3 inches (5 to 8 cm) wide but are endlessly
mesmerizing with their pink edges and lilac
undertones.

The Mill on the Floss has more than a
hundred petals on each bloom, with a sweet
button of a center. This bushy shrub is very
vigorous and grows to about 4 by 4 feet (1.2 by
1.2 m) with little pink cups dancing about the
foliage.

It has a slightly sweet, fruity fragrance, but
the big draw for Mill on the Floss is its one-of-
a-kind bloom shading that is unlike any other
rose.

BASICS

ROSE TYPE:	English shrub
BREEDER:	David Austin
COLOR:	Pink
FRAGRANCE:	Light
BLOOM FORM:	Cupped, rosette
PETAL COUNT:	100-plus
GROWTH TYPE:	Shrub
BLOOM TIME:	Repeat

PLANTING

PLANTING SEASON:	Spring
LIGHT REQUIREMENTS:	Full sun
HARDINESS ZONES:	5 to 10
SPACING:	4 feet (1.2 m)
HEIGHT:	4 feet (1.2 m)
WIDTH:	4 feet (1.2 m)
DISEASE RESISTANCE:	Excellent
CONTAINER PLANTING:	No

THERE IS A REASON FRANCIS MEILLAND has won numerous awards—including being named the 2013 winner of the All-America Rose Selections, a prestigious annual honor that recognized exceptional new rose varieties. Its intoxicating fragrance and large blooms stand out among other roses. Francis Meilland is a personal favorite and beloved by Grace Rose Farm's clients. Of the hundreds of varieties we grow on our farm, Francis Meilland has the longest vase life, which culminates in the petals opening to an impressive width.

This stunning rose was bred by Alain Meilland and was lovingly named after his father, a renowned French horticulturalist. The Meilland family founded their rose-growing business in 1850 and is known the world over for their rose varieties, with more than a thousand patents to their name.

As a remarkably tall and wide plant with lush green foliage, it makes for a perfect hedge. While Francis Meilland can bloom several times throughout the season, it does have a period where the flush distinctly ends and the plant refreshes to put on new growth.

BASICS

ROSE TYPE:	Hybrid tea
BREEDER:	Meilland
COLOR:	Blush to white
FRAGRANCE:	Strong
BLOOM FORM:	Cupped
PETAL COUNT:	50 to 80
GROWTH TYPE:	Hedge/upright
BLOOM TIME:	Repeat

PLANTING

PLANTING SEASON:	Spring
LIGHT REQUIREMENTS:	Full sun
HARDINESS ZONES:	5 to 9
SPACING:	4 feet (1.2 m)
HEIGHT:	5 to 7 feet (1.5 to 2.1 m)
WIDTH:	3 to 4 feet (0.9 to 1.2 m)
DISEASE RESISTANCE:	Excellent
CONTAINER PLANTING:	No

· EUSTACIA VYE ·

THE FIRST TIME I LAID EYES ON THIS
rose in person was at the Chelsea Flower Show,
and my excitement was beyond measure. David
Austin introduced Eustacia Vye in 2019 as part
of their literary collection, and it is named after
the heroine in Thomas Hardy's *The Return of
the Native*. Known to be a great cutting rose, it
has proven to be a wonderful, prolific addition
to our farm.

Eustacia Vye is an especially beautiful shrub
rose and no other English rose quite resembles
it. The flower softly radiates an apricot-pink
shade across its buttery face, and every bloom
is delicately ruffled. You cannot help but smile
when Eustacia Vye is flushing with its richly
hued petals that gradually fade over time.

This newly bred variety is very healthy and
will require little maintenance. David Austin
has perfected their breeding so their most
modern varieties will grow freely in nearly
every climate. Whether planted in a large
container or along a border, Eustacia Vye will
produce vivid, bountiful blooms from summer
to first frost. Being a medium-sized shrub,
Eustacia Vye is well suited for the front of the
garden bed. This variety is especially beautiful
when planted with lavender and other soft
herbs that will complement its sweet-scented
petals.

BASICS

ROSE TYPE:	English shrub
BREEDER:	David Austin
COLOR:	Mid-pink to apricot
FRAGRANCE:	Strong
BLOOM FORM:	Rosette
PETAL COUNT:	90
GROWTH TYPE:	Medium shrub
BLOOM TIME:	Repeat

PLANTING

PLANTING SEASON:	Spring
LIGHT REQUIREMENTS:	Full sun
HARDINESS ZONES:	4 to 11
SPACING:	3 feet (0.9 m)
HEIGHT:	4 feet (1.2 m)
WIDTH:	3 feet (0.9 m)
DISEASE RESISTANCE:	Excellent
CONTAINER PLANTING:	Yes

· EDEN ·

IF YOUR GARDEN HAS ROOM FOR JUST A single climber, it's a simple choice: Eden. Eden is an old-world charmer bred in 1985 by the house of Meilland in France with full, deeply cupped blooms that are creamy white, with prominent pink edging and hints of yellow. Named Pierre de Ronsard in France after the French poet by the same name, this rose was voted World's Favorite Rose by the World Federation of Rose Societies in 2006.

I love this rose so deeply. It offers an old-fashioned look with all the benefits of modern breeding: disease resistance, repeat blooming, and hardiness. I have never seen another rose flower so prolifically in the spring, and it will repeat nicely all summer. Eden's ruffled blossoms have seventy to one hundred petals and are borne in clusters. And as beautiful as Eden's blooms are, they are also extremely hardy and long-lasting.

One of the most vigorous climbing roses ever hybridized, Eden is the perfect choice for an archway, trellis, or gazebo. This is a versatile climber that can cover just about any structure. It is a vigorous rose that will spread and grow quickly, but it can also be kept manageable.

BASICS

ROSE TYPE:	Climbing
BREEDER:	Meilland
COLOR:	Cream to pink
FRAGRANCE:	Mild
BLOOM FORM:	Cupped
PETAL COUNT:	70 to 100
GROWTH TYPE:	Climbing
BLOOM TIME:	Repeat

PLANTING

PLANTING SEASON:	Spring
LIGHT REQUIREMENTS:	Full sun
HARDINESS ZONES:	5 to 11
SPACING:	5 feet (1.5 m)
HEIGHT:	Up to 12 feet (3.7 m)
WIDTH:	4 feet (1.2 m)
DISEASE RESISTANCE:	Excellent
CONTAINER PLANTING:	No

THIS GEM OF A ROSE IS COVETED BY home gardeners, rose farmers, and florists alike. Evelyn is known throughout the rose world as one of David Austin's masterpieces, and if you've never had an opportunity to experience this rose in person, you must. Not only is it stunning in appearance, but when you're close enough to take in this variety's perfume, it can leave you speechless. No other rose on our farm draws as much attention as Evelyn. It brings us so much joy to watch people marvel at its beauty during tours and farm visits.

As one of David Austin's older varieties, Evelyn can prove to be a bit high maintenance when it comes to disease prevention. However, the prolific, large blooms with apricot and pink petals and the intoxicating, fruity fragrance make it worth the effort. The long canes, which can easily bear up to a dozen blooms at a time, can become unruly if not maintained. The weight of all these flowers often pushes the canes toward the ground, so we recommend staking this plant.

BASICS

ROSE TYPE:	English shrub
BREEDER:	David Austin
COLOR:	Light pink to peach
FRAGRANCE:	Strong
BLOOM FORM:	Cupped
PETAL COUNT:	120-plus
GROWTH TYPE:	Arching shrub or medium climber
BLOOM TIME:	Repeat

PLANTING

PLANTING SEASON:	Spring
LIGHT REQUIREMENTS:	Full sun
HARDINESS ZONES:	5 to 10
SPACING:	4 to 5 feet (1.2 to 1.5 m)
HEIGHT:	6 feet (1.8 m)
WIDTH:	4 to 5 feet (1.2 to 1.5 m)
DISEASE RESISTANCE:	Moderate
CONTAINER PLANTING:	No

· COLETTE ·

COLETTE HAS THE MOST BEAUTIFUL, dainty, ballet-pink rosettes. Bred by Meilland in France, Colette is zoned 5 to 10, offering surprising hardiness given its delicate, romantic blooms. This is a light pink rose with warm apricot undertones that make it pop more in the garden than a traditional soft pink. Though it is a modern breed, Colette has an old-rose feel and gives off a musky, spicy, deep fragrance.

Colette's blooms open to about 3 to 3.5 inches (8 to 9 cm), which is an average size, but the plant is very prolific and blooms often. Because of its vigor and health, this rose will easily cover an arbor, trellis, or other architectural surface quickly in one season. While Colette is a climber, it can be grown as a shrub, but would need to be cut back often to keep it mannerly.

BASICS

ROSE TYPE:	Climbing shrub
BREEDER:	Meilland
COLOR:	Blush pink
FRAGRANCE:	Mild
BLOOM FORM:	Old-fashioned
PETAL COUNT:	135 to 140
GROWTH TYPE:	Climbing
BLOOM TIME:	Repeat

PLANTING

PLANTING SEASON:	Spring
LIGHT REQUIREMENTS:	Full sun
HARDINESS ZONES:	5 to 10
SPACING:	3 feet (0.9 m)
HEIGHT:	3 to 7 feet (0.9 to 2.1 m)
WIDTH:	3 feet (0.9 m)
DISEASE RESISTANCE:	Excellent
CONTAINER PLANTING:	No

MOONLIGHT IN PARIS IS A BEAUTIFUL French floribunda that we added to our farm several years ago when it became available in the United States. This aptly named rose exudes romance. Like a hydrangea, the blooms appear in a stunning variety of pastel colors that are impacted by soil conditions (acidity) and climate. For instance, in mild, consistent temperatures the blooms will be a soft blush to peach; when it is very hot, they can turn nearly white. In cool weather, the flower's tones will appear more saturated. It is a rather compact plant that blooms in huge sprays all season long. Ours have taken off quickly and flush reliably. Since Moonlight in Paris is a floribunda, there are always a few flowers to be harvested from the plants, even when the rose isn't in a flush. In the spring this charming rose is completely covered with sprays of 3- to 4-inch (8 to 10 cm) blossoms.

Moonlight in Paris's ruffled petals are held in a cup-shaped bloom, reminiscent of old garden roses, but with a more subtle fragrance. Many of the old-fashioned-shaped roses grow to be such large plants, but not Moonlight in Paris. It is a wonderful option for container gardening and small spaces. Planted in groupings or a hedge, Moonlight in Paris will put on a magnificent show and stay manageable at the same time.

The three-to-five-day vase life of Moonlight in Paris is fantastic and surprising, given how soft and fluttery its petals are. Its stems are straight, very hardy, and not too prickly. Moonlight in Paris is an excellent choice to add a touch of romance in a garden with limited space.

BASICS

ROSE TYPE:	Floribunda
BREEDER:	Delbard
COLOR:	Pale pink to peach with hints of yellow
FRAGRANCE:	Mild
BLOOM FORM:	Cupped
PETAL COUNT:	24 to 40
GROWTH TYPE:	Shrub
BLOOM TIME:	Repeat

PLANTING

PLANTING SEASON:	Spring
LIGHT REQUIREMENTS:	Full sun
HARDINESS ZONES:	6 to 9
SPACING:	4 feet (1.2 m)
HEIGHT:	4 to 5 feet (1.2 to 1.5 m)
WIDTH:	3 to 4 feet (0.9 to 1.2 m)
DISEASE RESISTANCE:	Good
CONTAINER PLANTING:	Yes

RESPLENDENT WITH PEACH AND APRICOT undertones, this is not your average pink rose. Bred by Meilland in France, Sweet Mademoiselle is a cabbage, old-world-style bloom with electric pink outer petals that swirl out of a bright apricot center. These colors will change with the seasons, resulting in deeper, more saturated tones in spring and fall and lighter shades in summer.

As the name suggests, Sweet Mademoiselle has a prominent fragrance, with lemon and grapefruit notes. It will grow well in Zones 5 to 11 and won an American Rose Society Award for Best Rose when it was first introduced in 2018. The distinction lauds this rose's disease resistance and prolific growing nature—it is a hybrid tea that blooms often and grows to be very large.

With full double blooms measuring 4.5 to 5 inches (11 to 13 cm) in diameter, this variety is great for cutting and bringing into the house to enjoy its impactful fragrance. Sweet Mademoiselle is best planted as a centerpiece rose and should be grown only in gardens that can accommodate its large size. Just one bush will take up plenty of space in the garden and serve as a striking focal rose.

BASICS

ROSE TYPE:	Hybrid Tea
BREEDER:	Meilland
COLOR:	Peachy pink
FRAGRANCE:	Strong
BLOOM FORM:	Old-fashioned
PETAL COUNT:	35-plus
GROWTH TYPE:	Upright
BLOOM TIME:	Repeat

PLANTING

PLANTING SEASON:	Spring
LIGHT REQUIREMENTS:	Full sun
HARDINESS ZONES:	5 to 10
SPACING:	4 feet (1.2 m)
HEIGHT:	5 feet (1.5 m)
WIDTH:	4 feet (1.2 m)
DISEASE RESISTANCE:	Excellent
CONTAINER PLANTING:	No

· BOSCOBEL ·

I AM A PINK ROSE LOVER THROUGH AND through, but my affinity for pink varieties did not come to light until I came across Boscobel. When we started our farm, I desperately wanted to grow all bright yellow, tangerine, watermelon, and saffron roses because those are the colors that bring me the most joy. I first saw this quintessential bright pink rose at Otto and Sons, my favorite local nursery, where it was in its glorious full spring bloom. The plant was three years old, and the flowers were massive—around 6 inches (15 cm) wide with seventy to eighty petals.

Boscobel's richly colored red buds open to cup-shaped, upward-facing rosettes in the sweetest salmon-pink shade. The darker buds create a beautiful contrast to the lighter blooms, and when open flowers and buds are present on the same stem, the effect is striking. Blooms sit atop the straight, erect stems, making this plant perfect for cutting. The rose's deep, rich aromas of myrrh, pear, almond, and licorice beautifully complement sweeter, brighter-scented roses in a bouquet.

Boscobel is a repeat bloomer, throwing out flowers all season long. It is not a massive bush; even in my Zone 10 climate it only reaches a maximum spread of 4 by 4 feet (1.2 by 1.2 m). The coral blooms pair beautifully with blue and purple flowers, such as salvia and lavender.

BASICS

ROSE TYPE:	English shrub
BREEDER:	David Austin
COLOR:	Salmon
FRAGRANCE:	Medium
BLOOM FORM:	Rosette
PETAL COUNT:	78
GROWTH TYPE:	Upright shrub
BLOOM TIME:	Repeat

PLANTING

PLANTING SEASON:	Spring
LIGHT REQUIREMENTS:	Full sun
HARDINESS ZONES:	5 to 11
SPACING	4 feet (1.2 m)
HEIGHT:	4 feet (1.2 m)
WIDTH:	4 feet (1.2 m)
DISEASE RESISTANCE:	Excellent
CONTAINER PLANTING:	No

LEONARDO DA VINCI IS A ROMANTIC floribunda rose with a gorgeous draping manner. Instead of its blooms pointing up to the sky with their heads facing the clouds, this rose nods gracefully, folding over itself with heavy 5- to 6-inch (10 to 13 cm) flowers. The fuchsia to raspberry flowers have blue undertones, giving them an unbelievable color that's fit for a painting.

Where some other roses have a looseness to the bloom, Leonardo da Vinci's many petals have an identical structure from one to the next. I can't help but think of the namesake artist's interests in both beauty and mathematics when I see this variety's blend of aesthetics and precision. This rose features seven or eight side buds around a central bud, with each flower head measuring an impressive size. The juxtaposition of the casual form of the plant and its sculptural, almost anatomical blooms is one of the qualities that makes this variety so special.

Bred by Meilland, Leonardo da Vinci makes a great cut flower, but the heads will nod because they are so heavy. Mixing this rose with a more erect variety will craft a beautiful arrangement or bouquet. In a vase, Leonardo da Vinci will cascade around and add interest to a more focal flower, like Francis Meilland (page 69). This elevated pink rose is also very fragrant, so it is sure to stun in both the garden and the vase.

BASICS

ROSE TYPE:	Floribunda
BREEDER:	Meilland
COLOR:	Pink
FRAGRANCE:	Mild
BLOOM FORM:	Quartered
PETAL COUNT:	75-plus
GROWTH TYPE:	Shrub
BLOOM TIME:	Repeat

PLANTING

PLANTING SEASON:	Spring
LIGHT REQUIREMENTS:	Full sun
HARDINESS ZONES:	5 to 10
SPACING:	4 feet (1.2 m)
HEIGHT:	4 to 5 feet (1.2 to 1.5 m)
WIDTH:	3 to 4 feet (0.9 to 1.2 m)
DISEASE RESISTANCE:	Excellent
CONTAINER PLANTING:	No

· SUMMER ROMANCE ·

BRED FOR A STRONG FRAGRANCE BY
Kordes for their Parfuma collection, Summer
Romance packs a strong, warm tea rose scent
with plenty of depth and spice notes. Typical
of floribundas, Summer Romance is highly
productive and blooms quickly and repetitively.

Since the rose tends to be rather compact,
it could be grown in a large container or serve
as a nice accent rose in the garden. A medium
pink with cool undertones, Summer Romance
would look pretty in a garden alongside other
cool-toned flowers like delphinium or lavender.

For gardeners looking for a gorgeous,
highly fragrant rose that doesn't take up much
space, this true pink rose is the perfect choice.

BASICS

ROSE TYPE:	Floribunda
BREEDER:	Kordes
COLOR:	Light pink
FRAGRANCE:	Strong
BLOOM FORM:	Quartered
PETAL COUNT:	75
GROWTH TYPE:	Bushy, upright
BLOOM TIME:	Repeat

PLANTING

PLANTING SEASON:	Spring
LIGHT REQUIREMENTS:	Full sun
HARDINESS ZONES:	5 to 11
SPACING:	4 feet (1.2 m)
HEIGHT:	4 feet (1.2 m)
WIDTH:	3 feet (0.9 m)
DISEASE RESISTANCE:	Good
CONTAINER PLANTING:	Yes

· DISTANT DRUMS ·

IMAGINE WALKING THROUGH A GARDEN overflowing with beautiful flowers when you come upon a rose with colors more captivating than any bloom you've ever seen. As a young bud Distant Drums appears pink, but as it slowly unfurls it reveals a rich copper center that fades to light blush. This variety is forever a favorite of rose enthusiasts, notable for its unforgettable light myrrh fragrance and blooms reminiscent of delicate water lilies.

Distant Drums is an upright and disease-resistant floribunda rose that produces single-stem blooms and magnificent clusters of ombré hues. It's usually the first plant in our garden to bloom each spring and is a generous repeat bloomer throughout the season. One mature plant can produce an unbelievable number of stems in a flush and can easily fill up many vases on its own. The foliage is a very healthy dark green, and in between flushes it puts on new growth in a contrasting shade of red. But beware, this bloom's unique beauty comes at a cost—it's one of the thorniest roses in our garden.

BASICS

ROSE TYPE:	Floribunda
BREEDER:	Dr. Griffith Buck
COLOR:	Copper center that fades to blush
FRAGRANCE:	Medium
BLOOM FORM:	High-centered
PETAL COUNT:	35 to 40
GROWTH TYPE:	Upright
BLOOM TIME:	Repeat

PLANTING

PLANTING SEASON:	Spring
LIGHT REQUIREMENTS:	Full sun
HARDINESS ZONES:	5 to 9
SPACING:	4 feet (1.2 m)
HEIGHT:	5 to 7 feet (1.5 to 2.1 m)
WIDTH:	3 to 4 (0.9 to 1.2 m)
DISEASE RESISTANCE:	Excellent
CONTAINER PLANTING:	No

· EMILY BRONTË ·

EMILY BRONTË IS A NEWER RELEASE from David Austin that we've been growing at the farm for a couple of seasons. An English shrub rose, this variety is sweet and dainty and reminds me of a little girl in a tutu. Loaded with 106 petals per bloom, Emily Brontë's heart unspools like a bolt of shimmery silk, a bright illumination of gold and apricot tones radiating from the center. Each ring of petals reaching outward from the heart fades to a lighter blush tone, eventually appearing almost translucent on the outer petals. The rose blooms out completely flat, putting all its dreamy petals on display and offering a delightful contrast to a cup-shaped rose.

Emily Brontë makes a nice accent among other, more prominent roses like hybrid teas or in a landscape among gardenias, azaleas, or hydrangeas. Its neutral shading will help it blend into any garden and would plant well with many other perennials. Emily Brontë will look lovely in a mixed border or as a hedge—the plant has a nice shape and does not spill over like other shrub roses. Because it is more manageable in size, Emily Brontë would also grow well in a pot or container.

I have Emily Brontë planted all over my front yard among peonies and other white and light blush flowers, and I enjoy its strong, old tea rose fragrance. As a cut rose it will last in the vase for three to four days.

BASICS

ROSE TYPE:	English shrub
BREEDER:	David Austin
COLOR:	Soft pink, apricot, cream
FRAGRANCE:	Strong
BLOOM FORM:	Cupped, rosette
PETAL COUNT:	106
GROWTH TYPE:	Shrub
BLOOM TIME:	Repeat

PLANTING

PLANTING SEASON:	Spring
LIGHT REQUIREMENTS:	Full sun
HARDINESS ZONES:	5 to 10
SPACING:	4 feet (1.2 m)
HEIGHT:	4 feet (1.2 m)
WIDTH:	3.5 feet (1.1 m)
DISEASE RESISTANCE:	Excellent
CONTAINER PLANTING:	Yes

I REFER TO THE ANCIENT MARINER AS my "happy accident." We received an order years ago from David Austin and somehow a dozen Ancient Mariner bushes snuck into the boxes, even though I hadn't ordered them. I tucked the bushes into our garden, and soon we were growing hundreds of these scene-stealing roses!

Its unique foliage appears hunter green but upon closer inspection tends toward mahogany tones with deep reds. The juxtaposition is striking when set against its bright pink blooms. The variety's name is inspired by Samuel Taylor Coleridge's epic poem "The Rime of the Ancient Mariner," which tells the tale of a sailor who has returned home from a long sea voyage. I can't help but wonder if this rose is the one David Austin could imagine welcoming home a weary traveler. It certainly lifts my spirits.

Unlike most roses that fade from outside in, the inner petals of the Ancient Mariner are the most saturated in a vibrant cotton candy pink. As the petals move outward, they soften to a pale, pinkish lilac to white. The Ancient Mariner blooms in clusters and singles; its massive single flower heads can reach 5 to 6 inches (13 to 15 cm) wide. The clusters offer smaller blooms but in great abundance. This plant is what I refer to as a house-eater in terms of size: It loves to spread its arms and grow long, weeping canes that can get to be 6 feet (1.8 m) long! While this might make it challenging for a formal garden space, with training it can be tamed. We let this rose grow wild on the farm because we have the space, and it produces masses of flowers steadily throughout the season.

BASICS

ROSE TYPE:	English shrub
BREEDER:	David Austin
COLOR:	Pink
FRAGRANCE:	Mild
BLOOM FORM:	Cupped
PETAL COUNT:	160
GROWTH TYPE:	Arching, large shrub
BLOOM TIME:	Repeat

PLANTING

PLANTING SEASON:	Spring
LIGHT REQUIREMENTS:	Full sun / partial shade
HARDINESS ZONES:	4 to 11
SPACING:	4 feet (1.2 m)
HEIGHT:	4 feet (1.2 m)
WIDTH:	4 feet (1.2 m)
DISEASE RESISTANCE:	Excellent
CONTAINER PLANTING:	No

THIS OPULENT ROSE WAS BRED IN
Germany by Kordes and is reminiscent of the
climber Eden (page 73). A compact rose and
not a climber, Blush Veranda possesses the
ravishing beauty of Eden with the feasibility
of being planted in a container—making it
accessible for those without a large garden
space. Though it only grows to be about 3 by
2 feet (0.9 by 0.6 m), this floribunda variety
is very hardy and could be described as a
workhorse of a plant.

This dainty rose blooms in clusters on
the plant, providing an abundance of delicate
flowers in a smaller scale. The quartered blush
blooms progress into creamy white-to-yellow
petals on the outer ring. Blush Veranda would
look sweet in a small garden or on a patio in a
classic urn.

BASICS

ROSE TYPE:	Floribunda
BREEDER:	Kordes
COLOR:	Pink
FRAGRANCE:	Mild
BLOOM FORM:	Quartered
PETAL COUNT:	65
GROWTH TYPE:	Upright
BLOOM TIME:	Repeat

PLANTING

PLANTING SEASON:	Spring
LIGHT REQUIREMENTS:	Full sun
HARDINESS ZONES:	5 to 11
SPACING:	3 feet (0.9 m)
HEIGHT:	3 feet (0.9 m)
WIDTH:	2 feet (0.6 m)
DISEASE RESISTANCE:	Very good
CONTAINER PLANTING:	Yes

· CANDICE ·

A STRIPED ROSE BRED BY DELBARD IN France, Candice is unlike any rose I've ever seen. Candice's heart is a creamy, peachy center that fades to a striped pink petal that looks like it's been delicately painted with watercolor. No two petals look alike, as each one displays a different striation. It's so beautiful it knocks your socks off.

Candice grows in impressive clusters and ranges in color from shades of gold to salmon, pink, and peach, making it somewhat of a chameleon. The buds start off a deep pink-to-red tone and reveal the varying sunset spectrum of hues as they open. This delightful variety does tend to fade in color once it is cut in the vase, resulting in a soothing pastel for its last stage.

BASICS

ROSE TYPE:	Shrub
BREEDER:	Delbard
COLOR:	Pink, cream, striped
FRAGRANCE:	Medium
BLOOM FORM:	Cupped
PETAL COUNT:	40
GROWTH TYPE:	Shrub
BLOOM TIME:	Repeat

PLANTING

PLANTING SEASON:	Spring
LIGHT REQUIREMENTS:	Full sun
HARDINESS ZONES:	5 to 10
SPACING:	3 feet (0.9 m)
HEIGHT:	2 to 3 feet (0.6 to 0.9 m)
WIDTH:	2 to 3 feet (0.6 to 0.9 m)
DISEASE RESISTANCE:	Excellent
CONTAINER PLANTING:	No

· OLIVIA ROSE AUSTIN ·

INTRODUCED IN 2014, OLIVIA ROSE
Austin is named after David Austin's
granddaughter. It is the most perfect ballet-
pink rose that you could imagine. Appearing
in clusters, the large blooms of light pink
petals are generally surrounded by smaller side
buds. Like a seasoned ballerina, the stems are
erect and fully support the astonishing flowers
floating over the lush green foliage.

Unlike some of David Austin's older
varieties of heavy-petaled roses, the blooms
of Olivia Rose Austin do not tend to ball in
cooler weather. In my experience, the buds are
not quite as globular as many English roses—
instead, they are pointed like a hybrid tea or
floribunda. Once they are fully open, however,
the blooms form a beautiful cup shape.

We planted several Olivia Rose Austin
plants in front of a bay window at our first
home. Just four months after planting, they had
filled out the window view and provided a mild
yet intoxicating aroma as the breeze came in.
In our warm climate, Olivia Rose Austin has
shown to be an excellent repeat bloomer and
is very disease resistant. This variety can be
grown close together and is perfect for hedges,
focal points, and containers.

BASICS

ROSE TYPE:	English shrub
BREEDER:	David Austin
COLOR:	Pink
FRAGRANCE:	Medium
BLOOM FORM:	Cupped
PETAL COUNT:	90
GROWTH TYPE:	Medium shrub
BLOOM TIME:	Repeat

PLANTING

PLANTING SEASON:	Spring
LIGHT REQUIREMENTS:	Partial sun
HARDINESS ZONES:	4 to 11
SPACING:	4 feet (1.2 m)
HEIGHT:	4.5 feet (1.4 m)
WIDTH:	3.5 feet (1.1 m)
DISEASE RESISTANCE:	Excellent
CONTAINER PLANTING:	Yes

· THE LADY GARDENER ·

THERE ARE NOT MANY ROSEBUSHES AS impressive and underrated as David Austin's The Lady Gardener. This variety's perfectly rounded shape with glossy green foliage and large ruffled petals ranging in color from apricot to pink makes it a standout. It can be a focal point in a garden bed and just as easily a lovely hedge, creating a dense border. The Lady Gardener is a prolific repeat bloomer, and a mature plant will produce dozens of stems each flush.

The quartered rosette blooms of The Lady Gardener can easily reach 4 to 5 inches (10 to 13 cm) in diameter. The hardy and straight stems hold up the flowers well, making this variety ideal for arranging. Along with this rose's great beauty, though, comes a trade-off: It has many, many thorns. Take great care when cutting this rose, bringing it into the home, or pruning its plants at the end of the season.

Thorns aside, The Lady Gardener is one of my favorite roses to harvest. The fragrance is entrancing, exuding a light tea scent with accents of cedarwood and vanilla. The vase life is excellent, and the blooms open much more slowly than most garden roses. David Austin dedicated this lovely rose to Plant Heritage, an organization that works diligently to protect Britain's garden plant diversity.

BASICS

ROSE TYPE:	English shrub
BREEDER:	David Austin
COLOR:	Peach to blush
FRAGRANCE:	Mild
BLOOM FORM:	Rosette
PETAL COUNT:	26 to 40
GROWTH TYPE:	Rounded shrub
BLOOM TIME:	Repeat

PLANTING

PLANTING SEASON:	Spring
LIGHT REQUIREMENTS:	Full sun
HARDINESS ZONES:	5 to 11
SPACING:	3 to 4 feet (0.9 to 1.2 m)
HEIGHT:	3 to 4 feet (0.9 to 1.2 m)
WIDTH:	3 to 4 feet (0.9 to 1.2 m)
DISEASE RESISTANCE	Excellent
CONTAINER PLANTING:	No

· PRINCESS ALEXANDRA OF KENT ·

THERE'S NO MISTAKING THE SUBLIME Princess Alexandra of Kent when strolling through the garden. This plant is an English shrub rose boasting a bushy shape that can easily go wild if left untamed, and it produces magnificent, large flowers. From a distance it appears as a bright pink bloom, but as you get closer, you'll notice a delicate blend of light and warm pink petals. The variation of pink tones and size of the petals are what make this rose so spectacular.

Princess Alexandra of Kent is one of David Austin's incredible creations. The enticing fragrance changes as the rose matures; when the petals just begin opening, the rose gives off a strong tea scent, and as they fully bloom the scent turns to a bright lemony aroma. The plant produces long, straight stems that make for excellent cut roses. The dense cup-shaped blossom has a vase life that can rival any true garden rose. This variety is also very disease resistant and hardy in cooler climates.

Besides having Princess Alexandra of Kent in our production field, we also have many plants located around our property mixed in with the landscape because they make a perfect hedge or border. This is one of our favorite roses to have around the house because the beautiful fragrance carries through our open windows on a breezy day. If you're looking to add an amazing pink bloom with strong fragrance to your home garden, it would be hard to pass up Princess Alexandra of Kent.

BASICS

ROSE TYPE:	English shrub
BREEDER:	David Austin
COLOR:	Pink
FRAGRANCE:	Strong
BLOOM FORM:	Cupped
PETAL COUNT:	130
GROWTH TYPE:	Large shrub
BLOOM TIME:	Repeat

PLANTING

PLANTING SEASON:	Spring
LIGHT REQUIREMENTS:	Full sun
HARDINESS ZONES:	5 to 9
SPACING:	4 feet (1.2 m)
HEIGHT:	3 to 4 feet (0.9 to 1.2 m)
WIDTH:	3 to 4 feet (0.9 to 1.2 m)
DISEASE RESISTANCE:	Excellent
CONTAINER PLANTING:	No

· PARIS DE YVES ST. LAURENT ·

THIS IS ONE OF THE FIRST ROSES I
started growing for Grace Rose Farm. In
both shading and structure, Paris de Yves
St. Laurent is unique. The color is a fusion
of pink, coral, and salmon, with blooms that
unwrap with a scalloped, oyster-shell effect
as they turn up and flutter open. The central
petal nearly covers the stamens and then
rolls outward, creating an almost undulating
movement from petal to petal.

A hybrid tea bred by Meilland in France,
this rose loves to bloom, is very disease
resistant, and has thick petals, making it an
ideal cut flower. Paris de Yves St. Laurent will
last for more than a week in a vase, allowing
you ample time to admire its eye-catching
bloom form.

BASICS

ROSE TYPE:	Hybrid tea
BREEDER:	Meilland
COLOR:	Pink
FRAGRANCE:	Mild
BLOOM FORM:	Cupped
PETAL COUNT:	35
GROWTH TYPE:	Upright
BLOOM TIME:	Repeat

PLANTING

PLANTING SEASON:	Spring
LIGHT REQUIREMENTS:	Full sun
HARDINESS ZONES:	7 to 10
SPACING:	4 feet (1.2 m)
HEIGHT:	4 feet (1.2 m)
WIDTH:	3 feet (0.9 m)
DISEASE RESISTANCE:	Excellent
CONTAINER PLANTING:	No

· MARC CHAGALL ·

DESCRIBED AS A PERFECT ROSE BY
several rosarians, Marc Chagall is a flower
like no other. I am not often a fan of striped
roses, but when I first saw Marc Chagall, I was
immediately taken aback by its striking beauty.
This prolific floribunda was named for the early
modernist Russian-French painter, and aptly so,
for its every bloom is like a painting: The pink
flowers are stroked with cream to pale yellow,
making each blossom truly individual.

True to its floribunda nature, Marc Chagall
is almost never out of bloom. Its pale green
leaves are the perfect backdrop for the richly
saturated blooms. It is a spectacular, jaw-
dropping rose with large, clustered flowers.

BASICS

ROSE TYPE:	Floribunda
BREEDER:	Delbard
COLOR:	Pink striped with cream, yellow
FRAGRANCE:	Mild
BLOOM FORM:	Cupped
PETAL COUNT:	30
GROWTH TYPE:	Compact
BLOOM TIME:	Repeat

PLANTING

PLANTING SEASON:	Spring
LIGHT REQUIREMENTS:	Full sun
HARDINESS ZONES:	5 to 10
SPACING:	3 to 4 feet (0.9 to 1.2 m)
HEIGHT:	3 feet (0.9 m)
WIDTH:	2 feet (0.6 m)
DISEASE RESISTANCE:	Excellent
CONTAINER PLANTING:	No

ONE OF THE DAINTIEST ROSES WE GROW, Queen of Sweden has ballet-pink petals that form a perfect cup-shaped bloom. As the sepals open, angelic globular buds unfurl into 2- to 3-inch (5 to 8 cm) rosettes. Though small and delicate, this David Austin rose is a charmer with a subtle myrrh fragrance.

If you don't have much room to garden, Queen of Sweden is an excellent choice because the plant is very upright. The cut stems are strong, straight, and relatively thornless with single blooms as well as stunning clusters. Queen of Sweden's foliage is another characteristic that makes this plant so unique: The leaves are round and matte green, unlike the pointed, glossy leaves of most roses. The plant can get very tall if left untamed but generally requires little maintenance and is extremely disease resistant.

Due to its diminutive bloom size, Queen of Sweden is more of an accent rose than a focal point and adds the perfect whimsy to any arrangement. For such a delicate flower, its vase life is longer than one would think: three to four days.

BASICS

ROSE TYPE:	English shrub
BREEDER:	David Austin
COLOR:	Ballet pink
FRAGRANCE:	Medium
BLOOM FORM:	Cupped
PETAL COUNT:	140
GROWTH TYPE:	Upright, bushy
BLOOM TIME:	Repeat

PLANTING

PLANTING SEASON:	Spring
LIGHT REQUIREMENTS:	Full sun
HARDINESS ZONES:	4 to 11
SPACING:	3 feet (0.9 m)
HEIGHT:	6 feet (1.8 m)
WIDTH:	3 feet (0.9 m)
DISEASE RESISTANCE:	Excellent
CONTAINER PLANTING:	No

· CÉCILE BRUNNER ·

FIRST INTRODUCED IN 1881 BY
Frenchman Pernet-Ducher, Cécile Brunner
is a climbing hybrid tea that has been very
popular with rose growers since the Victorian
era. Cécile Brunner is a quintessential cottage
countryside rose. It is an easy-to-maintain
plant widely used to create hedges and barriers.
If you were to plant a fence with this rose, it
would cover the structure in two years' time
in most climates. At our farm we planted
four Cécile Brunner roses to cover two stone
walls. Within one growing season, they had
completely covered the stone and made our
entrance undeniably charming.

Cécile Brunner has petite flowers, an
evocative sweet scent, a dainty form, and
long, cuttable stems. It is one of the very first
to bloom in the spring and will repeat in the
summer after deadheading. The 2-inch (5 cm),
fully double flowers arise from pointed buds,
with soft pink exteriors and a deeper pink
center. The fragrance is fruity and long-
lasting, never overpowering, but noticeably rich
with rose notes. Cécile Brunner is very long
blooming, delivering armloads of miniature
delights over many weeks.

BASICS

ROSE TYPE:	Climbing
BREEDER:	Pernet-Ducher
COLOR:	Blush pink
FRAGRANCE:	Medium
BLOOM FORM:	Rosette
PETAL COUNT:	17 to 25
GROWTH TYPE:	Climbing
BLOOM TIME:	Repeat

PLANTING

PLANTING SEASON:	Spring
LIGHT REQUIREMENTS:	Full sun
HARDINESS ZONES:	5 to 10
SPACING:	5 feet (1.5 m)
HEIGHT:	8 to 10 feet (2.4 to 3 m)
WIDTH:	2 to 4 feet (0.6 to 1.2 m)
DISEASE RESISTANCE:	Very good
CONTAINER PLANTING:	No

• ALNWICK ROSE •

THE BREATHTAKING AND REGAL
Alnwick Rose was one of my early favorites
and is a splendidly rounded and bushy plant.
By the second or third year in the ground,
once the plant has had time to mature, it will
bloom vigorously all season long. You'll never
stop cutting! And the number of blooms on the
Alnwick Rose is astounding. Its bright, cup-
shaped buds gradually open to full-petaled,
pinkish-coral cupped blooms.

Alnwick's luscious color reminds me of a
perfectly juicy summer watermelon. The tips
of the petals are lighter than the inside of the
bloom, creating a stunning ombré effect. The
matte foliage offers a lovely contrast to the
cheerful blooms. In addition, it has an old-
rose scent, with a bit of a fruity undertone,
reminiscent of raspberries.

The Alnwick Rose stays compact, rounded,
and upright, and although it is a hearty plant,
its smaller size makes it a perfect fit for a large
container. It is such a charming rose that no
matter how much gardening space you have, I
would strongly suggest making room for the
Alnwick.

BASICS

ROSE TYPE:	English shrub
BREEDER:	David Austin
COLOR:	Soft pink
FRAGRANCE:	Medium
BLOOM FORM:	Cupped
PETAL COUNT:	120
GROWTH TYPE:	Medium shrub / upright
BLOOM TIME:	Repeat

PLANTING

PLANTING SEASON:	Spring
LIGHT REQUIREMENTS:	Full sun
HARDINESS ZONES:	5 to 10
SPACING:	4 feet (1.2 m)
HEIGHT:	4 feet (1.2 m)
WIDTH:	3 feet (0.9 m)
DISEASE RESISTANCE:	Excellent
CONTAINER PLANTING:	Yes

GABRIEL OAK IS A NEWER DAVID AUSTIN rose, introduced in the US in 2019. This variety has a bold, fuchsia-raspberry color that seems to intensify the longer you look at it. David Austin named this English shrub rose after a character in the Thomas Hardy novel *Far from the Madding Crowd.*

The blooms on this plant are quartered and very big, though the plant itself does not grow to be too large. The outer petals fade to a lighter color than the rich, almost button nose of a center, creating a beautiful ombré effect. Gabriel Oak is a spotlight rose and should be planted as a focal point in the garden: Its striking blooms are best positioned along a pathway or somewhere they can get plenty of attention.

Gabriel Oak's fragrance matches its strong coloring. With a powerful fruity to citrusy fragrance, this variety is a star in the garden.

BASICS

ROSE TYPE:	English shrub
BREEDER:	David Austin
COLOR:	Deep pink
FRAGRANCE:	Strong
BLOOM FORM:	Rosette
PETAL COUNT:	125-plus
GROWTH TYPE:	Shrub
BLOOM TIME:	Repeat

PLANTING

PLANTING SEASON:	Spring
LIGHT REQUIREMENTS:	Full sun
HARDINESS ZONES:	5 to 10
SPACING:	4 feet (1.2 m)
HEIGHT:	4 feet (1.2 m)
WIDTH:	4 feet (1.2 m)
DISEASE RESISTANCE:	Excellent
CONTAINER PLANTING:	Yes

· YVES PIAGET ·

POSSIBLY THE WORLD'S MOST BELOVED cut rose, Yves Piaget is in a class all its own. It was named for the famous Swiss clockmaker, who crafts the trophy for the best variety in the Geneva rose competition, and has an old-fashioned form and rich color. This is an award-winning rose with timeless appeal.

Yves Piaget's scent is sunny citrus mixed with tea rose, and its long-lasting aroma will fill a room. The uniquely ruffled petals start out raspberry and fade as they open, with the bloom unfurling to 6 inches (15 cm) wide.

In our Mediterranean climate, Yves Piaget can be susceptible to powdery mildew. And often, the blooms are so dense they can have a hard time opening in moist climates. Yves Piaget has its best bloom of the season when conditions are warm and dry, though it's extraordinary any time of the growing season.

BASICS

ROSE TYPE:	Hybrid tea
BREEDER:	Meilland
COLOR:	Deep pink
FRAGRANCE:	Strong
BLOOM FORM:	Cupped
PETAL COUNT:	80
GROWTH TYPE:	Short bush
BLOOM TIME:	Repeat

PLANTING

PLANTING SEASON:	Spring
LIGHT REQUIREMENTS:	Full sun
HARDINESS ZONES:	6 to 10
SPACING:	3 to 4 feet (0.9 to 1.2 m)
HEIGHT:	3 feet (0.9 m)
WIDTH:	2 to 3 feet (0.6 to 0.9 m)
DISEASE RESISTANCE:	Good
CONTAINER PLANTING:	No

· JAMES GALWAY ·

DAVID AUSTIN NAMES MOST OF HIS ROSES after notable English figures. This beautiful rose, named after the renowned British flautist, holds a special place in my heart because I play the flute. It was quite possibly the first rose I ever grew when I started my garden.

A behemoth of a climber, this is not the rose for you if you don't have ample space. I've been in gardens where I've seen a single James Galway plant cover an entire terrace. Train this rose on a large arch and it will be enveloped in no time at all!

James Galway's slightly domed blooms are pink at the center, gradually becoming lighter blush to cream toward the edges. When the flowers are open, they flatten out completely, so you can see the gradation of ombré hues. This rose flushes in huge sprays that are lovely in the vase and quite long lasting. James Galway's scent is not as noteworthy as some other David Austin English roses, but it is distinctly old rose. The best time to enjoy James Galway is spring, when the plant is vigorous and produces many roses.

BASICS

ROSE TYPE:	English climbing
BREEDER:	David Austin
COLOR:	Pink ombré
FRAGRANCE:	Mild
BLOOM FORM:	Rosettes
PETAL COUNT:	130
GROWTH TYPE:	Climbing
BLOOM TIME:	Repeat

PLANTING

PLANTING SEASON:	Spring
LIGHT REQUIREMENTS:	Full sun
HARDINESS ZONES:	4 to 11
SPACING:	6 feet (1.8 m)
HEIGHT:	12 feet (3.7 m)
WIDTH:	4 feet (1.2 m)
DISEASE RESISTANCE:	Excellent
CONTAINER PLANTING:	No

· ASHLEY ·

BRED BY THE GERMAN BREEDER TANTAU, Ashley is a hybrid tea that shows exceptional hardiness for colder climates.

One of the things I most love about Ashley is the heart of the bloom. The quartered heart unravels into frilly, scalloped layered petals that form large pink flowers. While the bloom starts out as a true pink, it fades as it opens, creating a heavenly transitional look as it ages. Ashley opens slowly, culminating in 4- to 5-inch (10 to 13 cm) round heads that are almost completely flat, with mesmerizing, ruffled ridges along the top of the petals.

It's easy to see why florists and commercial growers choose this variety for weddings and other events. Ashley has an outstanding vase life, and because the buds are so tight, the petals don't fall off, even as it opens. I have enjoyed this rose in my home for more than ten days, admiring the staggeringly large, petal-packed heads for each one of them.

BASICS

ROSE TYPE:	Hybrid tea
BREEDER:	Tantau
COLOR:	Pink
FRAGRANCE:	Mild
BLOOM FORM:	Old-fashioned, rosette
PETAL COUNT:	118
GROWTH TYPE:	Upright
BLOOM TIME:	Repeat

PLANTING

PLANTING SEASON:	Spring
LIGHT REQUIREMENTS:	Full sun
HARDINESS ZONES:	5 to 9
SPACING:	4 feet (1.2 m)
HEIGHT:	3 to 4 feet (0.9 to 1.2 m)
WIDTH:	4 feet (1.2 m)
DISEASE RESISTANCE:	Excellent
CONTAINER PLANTING:	Yes

· NEW DAWN ·

NEW DAWN IS A VARIETY FROM 1930 that is still around today, a testament to its disease resistance and hardiness. This tried-and-true pale pink rose will climb anything it is affixed to, making it a staple for landscapers, landscape architects, or anyone needing to cover a large structure with roses.

New Dawn is a vigorous repeat bloomer and grows to be so massive (up to 20 feet/6.1 m tall) that if you wanted to cover an entire pergola, you could do so with just one plant on either side. This rose wants to bloom and does so over a short period of time. The flowers have a pale pink heart that fades open to white, creating a whimsical, romantic aesthetic. The wispy and fluttery blooms feature a lower petal count than other varieties but serve as a solid cut rose because of their long stems.

Whether you want a cottage garden look with a loose climbing rose or a rose climbing over a specific architectural piece to serve as a focal point, New Dawn will not disappoint. With its easy-to-manage nature, fast growth, and disease resistance, you don't have to be a seasoned rose grower to plant and enjoy New Dawn in your yard.

BASICS

ROSE TYPE:	Climbing
BREEDER:	Dreer
COLOR:	Pink
FRAGRANCE:	Strong
BLOOM FORM:	Old-fashioned
PETAL COUNT:	40
GROWTH TYPE:	Climbing
BLOOM TIME:	Repeat

PLANTING

PLANTING SEASON:	Spring
LIGHT REQUIREMENTS:	Full sun
HARDINESS ZONES:	4 to 10
SPACING:	12 feet (3.7 m)
HEIGHT:	15 to 20 feet (4.6 to 6.1 m)
WIDTH:	10 feet (3 m)
DISEASE RESISTANCE:	Excellent
CONTAINER PLANTING:	No

· JASMINA ·

PERHAPS MY FAVORITE THING ABOUT
Jasmina is the fluttery, wispy look of this plant's
loose petals as they blow in a gentle breeze.
While this variety has soft blooms, they hold
on to the plant for weeks—and if they are not
harvested, the sun will fade the petals, giving a
wonderful ombré effect.

This continuously flowering plant is always
covered in blossoms and will offer roses from
spring well into the fall. Jasmina's cupped pink
blooms are lightly fragrant of apples, a cheery
complement to the variety's delicate petals.

Jasmina would look beautiful in a garden
where you want a loose, informal-looking rose
that drapes over an arch or structure.

BASICS

ROSE TYPE:	Climbing
BREEDER:	Kordes
COLOR:	Pink
FRAGRANCE:	Mild
BLOOM FORM:	Rosette
PETAL COUNT:	50
GROWTH TYPE:	Climbing
BLOOM TIME:	Repeat

PLANTING

PLANTING SEASON:	Spring
LIGHT REQUIREMENTS:	Full sun
HARDINESS ZONES:	5 to 10
SPACING:	4 to 5 feet (1.2 to 1.5 m)
HEIGHT:	6 to 7 feet (1.8 to 2.1 m)
WIDTH:	3 to 4 feet (0.9 to 1.2 m)
DISEASE RESISTANCE:	Excellent
CONTAINER PLANTING:	No

· KISS ME KATE ·

KISS ME KATE IS A PINK CLIMBING ROSE
that has lovely quartered blooms packed with
cotton candy–hued petals. While this rose has a
classic bud shape with old-fashioned charm, it is
very disease resistant and vigorous.

Kiss Me Kate is known for being a reliable
climber, so it will cover a structure quickly.
This variety grows on long stems, making
it ideal for cutting and bringing into the
home. Kiss Me Kate's strong fragrance of
apple and raspberry will fill your spaces with
an intoxicating aroma while you take in the
blooms' splendor.

BASICS

ROSE TYPE:	Climbing
BREEDER:	Kordes
COLOR:	Pink
FRAGRANCE:	Strong
BLOOM FORM:	Quartered
PETAL COUNT:	40 to 60
GROWTH TYPE:	Climbing
BLOOM TIME:	Repeat

PLANTING

PLANTING SEASON:	Spring
LIGHT REQUIREMENTS:	Full sun
HARDINESS ZONES:	5 to 9
SPACING:	4 to 5 feet (1.2 to 1.5 m)
HEIGHT:	10 feet (3 m)
WIDTH:	4 feet (1.2 m)
DISEASE RESISTANCE:	Excellent
CONTAINER PLANTING:	No

PURPLE

and

MAUVE

I'M NOT MUCH OF A PURPLE PERSON—
it's my least favorite color—but I love this rose.
I planted this variety next to my bedroom,
where I can see and smell it daily. The buds on
this floribunda are a dark purple when they're
just starting to open, and when the bloom
unfurls it appears in a lighter orchid-purple hue.
Plum Perfect has a quartered, old-fashioned
center and grows in sprays.

In my experience, this rose, bred in
Germany by Kordes, is one of the hardier
purple varieties (purple-hued roses tend to be
weaker than pink or yellow roses). We have
four hundred Plum Perfect plants on our farm,
and I've never seen one have a problem. With
its plummy, velvety violet coloring and rich
foliage, this disease-resistant rose will look
beautiful and stand up to the elements in many
gardens.

BASICS

ROSE TYPE:	Floribunda
BREEDER:	Kordes
COLOR:	Purple
FRAGRANCE:	Mild
BLOOM FORM:	Quartered, old-fashioned
PETAL COUNT:	75
GROWTH TYPE:	Upright
BLOOM TIME:	Repeat

PLANTING

PLANTING SEASON:	Spring
LIGHT REQUIREMENTS:	Full sun
HARDINESS ZONES:	5 to 10
SPACING:	4 feet (1.2 m)
HEIGHT:	4 feet (1.2 m)
WIDTH:	3 feet (0.9 m)
DISEASE RESISTANCE:	Excellent
CONTAINER PLANTING:	No

• LOVE SONG •

THIS IS THE BEST CUT LAVENDER ROSE
I've ever grown. Lavender-toned roses tend not
to have the vigor of the pinks, whites, and reds,
in part because of a different genetic profile.
However, Love Song, a Weeks Roses variety
bred by Tom Carruth, defies the odds. Purple
roses have made a comeback with florists, and
I think Love Song has a lot to do with their
newfound popularity.

As a rule of thumb, the hardier the rose, the
lighter the fragrance, and this is true with Love
Song. What it lacks in scent, however, it makes
up for in beauty and size. The bloom weight is
incredible, so much so that we must stake these
plants in the spring, though its largest flowers
appear in the cooler fall weather. Its petals are
thick and sturdy, and its straight, erect stems,
while quite thorny, are thick and take up water
abundantly, meaning this variety has a long
vase life.

In our warm, dry climate this floribunda
plant will form a 4- by 3-foot (1.2 by 0.9 m)
rounded shrub, with sprays of massive English-
style cabbage roses. Love Song offers an
antique, old-world, romantic rose with the
conveniences of modern breeding in that it
has excellent disease resistance. In the garden,
it pairs beautifully with silvery foliage such
as dusty miller and lamb's ear. This rose is
covered in buds and blossoms all season long.
It takes a little longer than some roses to
produce its blooms because the plant puts so
much energy into growing its massive flowers.
The petals are swirled with layers of deeper
lavender to periwinkle, light lilac to mauve,
though in the height of the season, this rose is a
true lavender.

BASICS

ROSE TYPE:	Floribunda
BREEDER:	Tom Carruth
COLOR:	Lavender
FRAGRANCE:	Mild
BLOOM FORM:	Cupped
PETAL COUNT:	41-plus
GROWTH TYPE:	Bushy, round
BLOOM TIME:	Repeat

PLANTING

PLANTING SEASON:	Spring
LIGHT REQUIREMENTS:	Full sun
HARDINESS ZONES:	5 to 10
SPACING:	4 feet (1.2 m)
HEIGHT:	4 feet (1.2 m)
WIDTH:	3 feet (0.9 m)
DISEASE RESISTANCE:	Excellent
CONTAINER PLANTING:	No

· DARCEY BUSSELL ·

THIS RICH, DEEP CRIMSON ROSE REMINDS me of a lush Burgundy wine. Although it has a slightly lower petal count than other David Austin roses, I love its whimsical, fluttery bloom form. Darcey Bussell is a large, bushy plant that can reach 5 by 5 feet (1.5 by 1.5 m). Its grass-green foliage is prone to powdery mildew, so make sure you stay on top of disease prevention to keep the plant healthy (for more on this, see pages 247–248).

Its blooms, which occur in both singles and sprays, sit at the top of straight stems and face upward with no bending or nodding. The deep wine color tends to stay very consistent, although in high heat the flowers can turn more red than burgundy. Not widely noted for its fragrance, this rose does nonetheless possess a very light, fruity scent. Darcey Bussell repeats quickly and the plants are always covered in buds or flowers, which is a treat in the garden.

Darcey Bussell's outer petals form a ring around the inner cup, and open to reveal a perfect rosette. However, this rose opens quickly, so we harvest it in the tightest form possible to extend the vase life. Our customers who receive this rose are often taken aback by the thumbprint-sized buds, but within a day or two of cutting, they open fully and enjoy a maximum vase life of five days. Because this variety doesn't produce a lot of thorns, this is a great rose for cutting and arranging.

BASICS

ROSE TYPE:	English shrub
BREEDER:	David Austin
COLOR:	Burgundy
FRAGRANCE:	Mild
BLOOM FORM:	Cupped
PETAL COUNT:	70
GROWTH TYPE:	Large shrub
BLOOM TIME:	Repeat

PLANTING

PLANTING SEASON:	Spring
LIGHT REQUIREMENTS:	Full sun
HARDINESS ZONES:	5 to 10
SPACING:	5 feet (1.5 m)
HEIGHT:	4 to 5 feet (1.2 to 1.5 m)
WIDTH:	3 to 4 feet (0.9 to 1.2 m)
DISEASE RESISTANCE:	Excellent
CONTAINER PLANTING:	No

· EBB TIDE ·

EBB TIDE IS A HANDSOME ROSE BRED BY Tom Carruth, a prolific rose hybridizer and the current curator of the rose collection at the famed Huntington Library in San Marino, California. In my opinion, this rose is one of his finest creations, as it has the unique ability to maintain its true plum color throughout almost the entire season. (Roses typically change color depending on the weather, but Ebb Tide holds on to its deep purple saturation even during the hot months.)

Once the plant is mature, the petal count is significant and the big, heavy blooms radiate with an intense fragrance. As the flower slowly opens, it reveals beautiful golden stamens that complement the purple petals. In our rose fields, Ebb Tide stands out as a distinctly sophisticated rose.

BASICS

ROSE TYPE:	Floribunda
BREEDER:	Tom Carruth
COLOR:	Violet
FRAGRANCE:	Strong
BLOOM FORM:	Old-fashioned
PETAL COUNT:	26 to 40
GROWTH TYPE:	Upright
BLOOM TIME:	Repeat

PLANTING

PLANTING SEASON:	Spring
LIGHT REQUIREMENTS:	Full sun
HARDINESS ZONES:	6 to 9
SPACING:	4 feet (1.2 m)
HEIGHT:	2 to 4 feet (0.6 to 1.2 m)
WIDTH:	4 feet (1.2 m)
DISEASE RESISTANCE:	Good
CONTAINER PLANTING:	No

WITH ITS INTENSE LILAC CENTER THAT blooms out to light lavender petals, Quicksilver is an old-fashioned–shaped climber that doesn't overpower the garden. Since it grows to about 7 to 8 feet (2.1 to 2.4 m) tall by 4 feet (1.2 m) wide, this rose climbs beautifully on a small arbor, trellis, or fence.

Quicksilver combines charm with modern breeding—it is disease resistant, healthy, and easy to maintain. The romantic double blooms of this rose and the sumptuous coloring make it look as though it's been growing for ages and is an antique rose, but it's not.

This charming variety will show different shading across the rosebush; a single cluster will have dark lilac buds and silvery open blooms. The result is a magnificent ombré effect across the entire bush.

BASICS

ROSE TYPE:	Climbing
BREEDER:	Kordes
COLOR:	Lavender to silver
FRAGRANCE:	Light
BLOOM FORM:	Old-fashioned
PETAL COUNT:	25
GROWTH TYPE:	Climbing
BLOOM TIME:	Repeat

PLANTING

PLANTING SEASON:	Spring
LIGHT REQUIREMENTS:	Full sun
HARDINESS ZONES:	5 to 9
SPACING:	4 feet (1.2 m)
HEIGHT:	7 to 8 feet (2.1 to 2.4 m)
WIDTH:	3 to 4 feet (0.9 to 1.2 m)
DISEASE RESISTANCE:	Good
CONTAINER PLANTING:	No

I WAS EXCITED TO PLANT THIS PURPLE rose, which is the child of Ebb Tide (page 124) and Grande Dame, bred by Christian Bédard at Weeks Roses. I had very high hopes that the rich, deep purple blooms would hold on to their color throughout the season, and I was not disappointed.

Celestial Night is a floribunda that grows in gorgeous sprays. While it doesn't have the largest flowers, there is one central bloom and a dozen outer, smaller ones. The stems can be easily cut apart into individual stems, but since the heads are on the smaller side, I prefer to keep them as one single stem. With the central blooms reaching about 3 to 4 inches (8 to 10 cm) wide when fully open, you'll need only three or so stems to fill a vase.

Celestial Night has beautifully healthy, dense foliage and is disease resistant. It makes for a great border rose when planted to create a full and bushy hedge. You can count on this plant to be an excellent repeater throughout the season.

BASICS

ROSE TYPE:	Floribunda
BREEDER:	Christian Bédard
COLOR:	Purple
FRAGRANCE:	Mild
BLOOM FORM:	Quartered, cupped
PETAL COUNT:	40
GROWTH TYPE:	Bushy
BLOOM TIME:	Repeat

PLANTING

PLANTING SEASON:	Spring
LIGHT REQUIREMENTS:	Full sun
HARDINESS ZONES:	5 to 9
SPACING:	4 feet (1.2 m)
HEIGHT:	4 feet (1.2 m)
WIDTH:	3 feet (0.9 m)
DISEASE RESISTANCE:	Excellent
CONTAINER PLANTING:	No

· STAINLESS STEEL ·

AS ITS NAME IMPLIES, THIS ROSE IS A silvery pastel lavender, with hardy petals. Of all the silver roses that have come to market, this is the most vigorous and healthy variety. Long-lasting petals are rare for roses in the blue family, but because of its excellent breeding, Stainless Steel is the best of the silver roses for growing as a cut flower.

Of all our roses, Stainless Steel produces the biggest canes at the base of the plant. These massive, tree-trunk-like canes hold up an impressively large plant: By the fall, this rosebush can reach 7 feet (2.1 m) tall, even with the heavy pruning that we do on the farm. Dark foliage beautifully complements the silvery lavender, pearl-like petals.

While Stainless Steel does produce single-stem roses too, it mostly blooms in luscious, full sprays that are easy to harvest and will fill a vase with the fruitiest, sweetest fragrance. A single spray, because of the low fork of the stem, can be cut as three to five stems. And one stem can fill an entire vase because it branches so beautifully. The massive heads, in their gentle pastel color, are spellbinding in the garden.

Stainless Steel's one drawback is that because of its light color, it tends to attract western flower thrips. Being proactive with pest control is key to having gorgeous blooms on Stainless Steel. For more on controlling pests like thrips, see page 243.

BASICS

ROSE TYPE:	Hybrid tea
BREEDER:	Tom Carruth
COLOR:	Mauve or purple blend
FRAGRANCE:	Strong
BLOOM FORM:	High-centered
PETAL COUNT:	25 to 30
GROWTH TYPE:	Upright
BLOOM TIME:	Repeat

PLANTING

PLANTING SEASON:	Spring
LIGHT REQUIREMENTS:	Full sun
HARDINESS ZONES:	7 to 10
SPACING:	4 feet (1.2 m)
HEIGHT:	5 to 7 feet (1.5 to 2.1 m)
WIDTH:	3 feet (0.9 m)
DISEASE RESISTANCE:	Good
CONTAINER PLANTING:	No

IF THERE'S ONE ROSE THAT HAS BEEN the most sought after by customers since the beginning of Grace Rose Farm, it's Koko Loko. This variety has a rich mocha color that fades to lavender and can be any variant in between, depending on weather conditions. The mocha is more vibrant during the cooler months, while in warmer weather the rose can be purely lavender. During the first flush of the season, it's not uncommon to see perfect swirls of mocha to caramel as the petals alternate color.

This plant is unique in its growth pattern. It will provide a dense layer of blooms on the bottom of the plant while it simultaneously puts on top growth. Just as the flowers on the bottom begin to slow down, the new top section grows vigorously in sprays. Koko Loko makes for a stunning cut flower as it produces both long, straight stems and stems with a nodding, whimsical feeling. They come in single-stem blossoms as well as magnificent clusters. Koko Loko is a special treat in the garden as its full, rounded shape makes for a spectacular focal point.

This rose's neutral tones can complement any bouquet, from a romantic bridal bouquet to a cheerful spring arrangement to a warm autumnal display. We have about two thousand of these plants on our farm, and it seems like we're always cutting every possible stem.

BASICS

ROSE TYPE:	Floribunda
BREEDER:	Christian Bédard
COLOR:	Mocha, taupe, lavender
FRAGRANCE:	Medium
BLOOM FORM:	Old-fashioned
PETAL COUNT:	30 to 35
GROWTH TYPE:	Round
BLOOM TIME:	Repeat

PLANTING

PLANTING SEASON:	Spring
LIGHT REQUIREMENTS:	Full sun
HARDINESS ZONES:	5 to 10
SPACING:	4 feet (1.2 m)
HEIGHT:	3 to 4 feet (0.9 to 1.2 m)
WIDTH:	3 to 4 feet (0.9 to 1.2 m)
DISEASE RESISTANCE:	Good
CONTAINER PLANTING:	No

CONNIE'S SANDSTORM WAS BRED BY A dear friend of ours, Burling Leong of Burlington Rose Nursery in California. Burling is a lover of oddball roses with colors not often well produced in the rose world, specifically, mustards and tans. Quality roses in this color family are not easy to breed. However, Burling found a beautiful cross between two roses that we already grow at our farm—Honey Dijon (page 191), a popular honey-toned rose, and Angel Face, a rose in the purple-mauve family. After crossing this rose, Burling trialed it for several years at her nursery in Central California, and then offered it to us. Grace Rose Farm became the first in the US to grow Connie's Sandstorm.

We loved it so much that we had Burling propagate hundreds of plants for us, and it is now in our production fields. Connie's Sandstorm has a striking color palette, with petals falling across the ombré spectrum from golden honey to rich mauve. This rose opens fully to reveal golden stamens.

The blooms' coloration is greatly impacted by the weather; in the spring, you'll notice much deeper tones, with the mauve tending toward the darker side. As the summer heat rolls in, the colors lighten up; the honey mustard moves toward tan, and the darker mauve slides into a lighter lavender. I love watching the changes and am constantly in awe of this rose's beauty.

BASICS

ROSE TYPE:	Floribunda
BREEDER:	Burling Leong
COLOR:	Tan-brown, mauve
FRAGRANCE:	Mild
BLOOM FORM:	High-centered
PETAL COUNT:	17 to 25
GROWTH TYPE:	Upright
BLOOM TIME:	Repeat

PLANTING

PLANTING SEASON:	Spring
LIGHT REQUIREMENTS:	Full sun
HARDINESS ZONES:	6 to 10
SPACING:	4 feet (1.2 m)
HEIGHT:	4 feet (1.2 m)
WIDTH:	3 to 4 feet (0.9 to 1.2 m)
DISEASE RESISTANCE:	Excellent
CONTAINER PLANTING:	No

RED

TOM CARRUTH, ROSE HYBRIDIZER extraordinaire and one of the most respected rosarians in the US, is a great friend of Grace Rose Farm and the breeder of this exceptional red rose. When I asked him to describe Hot Cocoa in a single sentence, he said, "It's all about the fade." The bloom color begins with sienna, a unique, smoky shade of red that lends itself beautifully to autumn-inspired arrangements. On the outer petals, purple undertones create a striking complement leading into the reds. As the rose matures and opens, it fades to a beautiful, almost translucent red. Its bright green, glossy foliage is an unexpected contrast to the deep tones of the blooms. Because of its striations and ombré effect, this rose's coloring can go with almost any arrangement palette, from soft pinks and creams to bold hot pinks and yellows.

This plant is remarkably tall for a floribunda and blooms in plentiful sprays. It is extremely thorny, so proceed with caution when planting, pruning, and harvesting this rose. If you have a neighbor who likes to steal your roses, I highly recommend planting a hedge of Hot Cocoa. It creates an almost impenetrable wall of wicked thorns!

Hot Cocoa, besides being ravishing, is cold weather–hardy, low maintenance, and disease resistant. Tom Carruth boasts that it is one of his healthiest, longest-living breeds. Along with Distant Drums (page 84), it is among the first to bloom in our fields each spring.

BASICS

ROSE TYPE:	Floribunda
BREEDER:	Tom Carruth
COLOR:	Burnt red, rust, russet
FRAGRANCE:	Mild
BLOOM FORM:	High-centered
PETAL COUNT:	30
GROWTH TYPE:	Upright, shrub
BLOOM TIME:	Repeat

PLANTING

PLANTING SEASON:	Spring
LIGHT REQUIREMENTS:	Full sun
HARDINESS ZONES:	5 to 10
SPACING:	4 feet (1.2 m)
HEIGHT:	5 feet (1.5 m)
WIDTH:	3 feet (0.9 m)
DISEASE RESISTANCE:	Excellent
CONTAINER PLANTING:	No

BLACK BACCARA'S DEEP, LUSCIOUS PETALS look astonishingly like actual velvet fabric. This is a high-drama, moody, and seductive rose that is unlike any other red variety.

Bred by Meilland in France, Black Baccara is zoned 5 to 9, but it performs well in my Zone 10 climate. Everything about this rose says luxury. The foliage is a deep, muddy green and the blooms each have forty-five to fifty petals that unfurl in the most romantic way. The petal edges of this dark red rose can often have a bit of a blackish shading.

Black Baccara, while breathtaking in color, also has an impressive vase life: a whopping ten to twelve days. This intense rose blooms all season long and will form a tall, bushy shrub you'll notice every time you pass by.

BASICS

ROSE TYPE:	Hybrid tea
BREEDER:	Meilland
COLOR:	Dark red, burgundy
FRAGRANCE:	Mild
BLOOM FORM:	High-centered
PETAL COUNT:	45 to 50
GROWTH TYPE:	Upright, bushy
BLOOM TIME:	Repeat

PLANTING

PLANTING SEASON:	Spring
LIGHT REQUIREMENTS:	Full sun
HARDINESS ZONES:	5 to 9
SPACING:	4 feet (1.2 m)
HEIGHT:	4 to 6 feet (1.2 to 1.8 m)
WIDTH:	3 feet (0.9 m)
DISEASE RESISTANCE:	Excellent
CONTAINER PLANTING:	No

· HEATHCLIFF ·

HEATHCLIFF IS A SPELLBINDING, magnificent crimson rose bred by David Austin. This beautiful English shrub rose has true red tones with a bit of dark raspberry and blue undertones. The blooms of Heathcliff could not be any fluffier or more ruffled, and they each contain a full petal count of more than one hundred petals, delivering big, dense blooms. The fragrance is a light old-rose scent, uplifting but not too strong.

Heathcliff will grow in an upright, bushy manner. As a shrub, the rose takes on a free-flowing, cottage-type form, but its crimson coloring would look beautiful with companion plants in purple, white, or light pink shades.

BASICS

ROSE TYPE:	Hybrid tea
BREEDER:	David Austin
COLOR:	Crimson
FRAGRANCE:	Light
BLOOM FORM:	Rosette
PETAL COUNT:	105 to 130
GROWTH TYPE:	Bushy, upright
BLOOM TIME:	Repeat

PLANTING

PLANTING SEASON:	Spring
LIGHT REQUIREMENTS:	Full sun
HARDINESS ZONES:	5 to 10
SPACING:	4 feet (1.2 m)
HEIGHT:	5 feet (1.5 m)
WIDTH:	3.5 feet (1.1 m)
DISEASE RESISTANCE:	Excellent
CONTAINER PLANTING:	No

TRAVIATA, BRED BY MEILLAND IN
France as part of their Romantica series, evokes
a classic red lipstick. There are no pink or
purple undertones to be found in this romantic
and sophisticated rose—just all red! I don't
usually gravitate to red roses, but because of
its old-rose style, deep cup-shaped flowers,
and plentiful ruffles, Traviata is the one true
red rose that stole my heart. It has so much
character, and its bright red hue set against
its glossy, deep green foliage make it an eye-
catching addition to any garden. It's also a
hardy, disease-resistant plant.

While this rose doesn't have a strong scent,
what it lacks in fragrance it makes up for in
vase life. Flowers last seven to nine days both
on the plant and in a vase due to the thick
stems, which take in ample water. Because of
the petals' deeply saturated color, they do tend
to burn if they stay on the plant for too long:
You'll want to harvest when the roses are
fully open, and put them in a vase out of direct
sunlight. One stem can fill an entire vase, as
each spray can measure 18 inches (46 cm) wide
with five or six blooms.

BASICS

ROSE TYPE:	Hybrid tea
BREEDER:	Meilland
COLOR:	Red
FRAGRANCE:	Mild
BLOOM FORM:	Old-fashioned
PETAL COUNT:	30
GROWTH TYPE:	Upright
BLOOM TIME:	Repeat

PLANTING

PLANTING SEASON:	Spring
LIGHT REQUIREMENTS:	Full sun
HARDINESS ZONES:	6 to 9
SPACING:	4 feet (1.2 m)
HEIGHT:	Up to 6 feet (1.8 m)
WIDTH:	4 feet (1.2 m)
DISEASE RESISTANCE:	Excellent
CONTAINER PLANTING:	No

· FIJI ELEGANZA

ON THE OPPOSITE END OF THE RED
range from Black Baccara (page 138), Fiji
Eleganza is a cherry-pink rose that brings a
pop of punchy color to the garden. The stems
of this hybrid tea rose feature a large center
blossom with sweet cluster blooms on the sides.
The flowers measure about 3 to 4 inches (8 to
10 cm) wide, and the cluster blooms help to
completely cover the plant in roses.

Bred by Kordes, this plant is mannerly and
will not take over the garden. Its light green
and glossy foliage are the perfect complement
to the delicious red hue. With a light fragrance,
this variety brings an effervescent energy inside
the home when it's placed in a vase.

BASICS

ROSE TYPE:	Hybrid tea
BREEDER:	Kordes
COLOR:	Cherry pink
FRAGRANCE:	Light
BLOOM FORM:	Old-fashioned
PETAL COUNT:	40
GROWTH TYPE:	Upright
BLOOM TIME:	Repeat

PLANTING

PLANTING SEASON:	Spring
LIGHT REQUIREMENTS:	Full sun
HARDINESS ZONES:	5 to 10
SPACING:	4 feet (1.2 m)
HEIGHT:	3 to 4 feet (0.9 to 1.2 m)
WIDTH:	3 feet (0.9 m)
DISEASE RESISTANCE:	Excellent
CONTAINER PLANTING:	No

OF SIMILAR CHARACTER TO A WILD rose, David Austin's Thomas à Becket has a natural, shrubby growth. Often when we think of red roses, formality comes to mind. This variety's striking, fully double crimson rosettes nod gently and attractively on their stems, giving them more of an informal quality. It is a vigorous plant that will grow freely and is quick to rebloom.

The old-rose fragrance of Thomas à Becket has a distinct lemon zest profile. In warmer regions or high summer, the flowers will take on a dark raspberry hue, while in cooler areas or in the spring and fall, blooms will be a true dark red. They resemble fluttery puffs and are quite prolific. This plant is easily manageable in the garden and looks especially beautiful when planted in groupings of three or five.

BASICS

ROSE TYPE:	English shrub
BREEDER:	David Austin
COLOR:	Crimson red
FRAGRANCE:	Medium
BLOOM FORM:	Rosette
PETAL COUNT:	63
GROWTH TYPE:	Large shrub
BLOOM TIME:	Repeat

PLANTING

PLANTING SEASON:	Spring
LIGHT REQUIREMENTS:	Full sun
HARDINESS ZONES:	5 to 11
SPACING:	4 feet (1.2 m)
HEIGHT:	5 feet (1.5 m)
WIDTH:	4 feet (1.2 m)
DISEASE RESISTANCE:	Good
CONTAINER PLANTING:	No

I CONSIDER MUNSTEAD WOOD TO BE THE flagship burgundy David Austin rose. This is a true English rose in every sense of the word, with cabbage-shaped blooms in clusters and singles and velvety petals that are stunningly intricate and heavily layered. Throughout the heat of the summer (except perhaps at the very height of a heat wave), it holds its deep, luscious wine color. The scent tends toward the classic old rose fragrance but with subtle fruity notes reminiscent of blackberries warming in the sun.

The plants tend to be on the smaller side, even in our hot climate—by midseason they reach their peak size of about 3 by 3 feet (0.9 by 0.9 m), which is petite for an English rose. Munstead Wood is a perfect choice for a smaller garden or a container garden. In fact, it can grow beautifully in a 15-gallon (57 L) pot.

We've grown so many burgundy and dark red roses—in many ways, I think of this color as an anchor in the garden. It's not fire-engine red or bright pink, so it blends into a landscape and is easy on the eye. Munstead Wood blooms abundantly and repeats quickly throughout the season, with five or six flushes. One drawback is that it's incredibly thorny, with thorns like little shark teeth all up and down the stems. They are unavoidable, so handle with care and always wear gloves. Some of the stems are very erect and thick and sit nicely upright in a vase, while others have a weepier quality and will spill over the rim.

BASICS

ROSE TYPE:	English shrub
BREEDER:	David Austin
COLOR:	Burgundy
FRAGRANCE:	Strong
BLOOM FORM:	Cupped
PETAL COUNT:	140-plus
GROWTH TYPE:	Shrub
BLOOM TIME:	Repeat

PLANTING

PLANTING SEASON:	Spring
LIGHT REQUIREMENTS:	Full sun
HARDINESS ZONES:	5 to 10
SPACING:	4 feet (1.2 m)
HEIGHT:	3 feet (0.9 m)
WIDTH:	3 feet (0.9 m)
DISEASE RESISTANCE:	Excellent
CONTAINER PLANTING:	Yes

· INGRID BERGMAN ·

LIKE ITS SWEDISH NAMESAKE, INGRID
Bergman is graceful and elegant. The large
fire-engine-red flowers can stop any passersby
in their tracks. When they are flushing, there's
nothing quite like the sea of deep red roses on
Ingrid Bergman's large, healthy plants. The
dark green foliage beautifully supports the pure
red blooms.

Created in Denmark, this multi-award-
winning hybrid tea was first introduced in
1984 and is arguably the bestselling red hybrid
tea rose because of its beauty and tolerance
for many different climates around the world.
The plant will grow to 5 feet (1.5 m) tall, is
extremely disease resistant, has a classic rose
fragrance, and bears very sturdy stems. The
blooms can open to a staggering 6 inches
(15 cm) wide and occur as single stems and
some sprays.

BASICS

ROSE TYPE:	Hybrid tea
BREEDER:	Poulsen
COLOR:	Dark red
FRAGRANCE:	None to mild
BLOOM FORM:	High-centered
PETAL COUNT:	30 to 35
GROWTH TYPE:	Upright
BLOOM TIME:	Repeat

PLANTING

PLANTING SEASON:	Spring
LIGHT REQUIREMENTS:	Full sun
HARDINESS ZONES:	4 to 10
SPACING:	4 feet (1.2 m)
HEIGHT:	5 feet (1.5 m)
WIDTH:	2 feet (0.6 m)
DISEASE RESISTANCE:	Excellent
CONTAINER PLANTING:	No

OKLAHOMA IS FAMOUS FOR BEING A tried-and-true, romantic red rose. A deeply dark red, this hybrid tea rose makes a wonderful cut flower. Its extraordinary tea fragrance is lusciously sweet, adding to the appeal of this absolute knockout of a rose.

Hybridized by Herbert Swim and O.L. Weeks at Oklahoma State University in 1964, the plant grows to be very bushy with substantial blooms that are more than 5 inches (13 cm) wide. Oklahoma is a very healthy variety that can grow to be 7 to 8 feet (2.1 to 2.4 m) tall in warm climates. It will serve the garden well as a focal, standout rose. It's a true showstopper.

BASICS

ROSE TYPE:	Hybrid tea
BREEDER:	Swim & Weeks
COLOR:	Red
FRAGRANCE:	Strong
BLOOM FORM:	High-centered
PETAL COUNT:	50
GROWTH TYPE:	Tall, upright, bushy
BLOOM TIME:	Repeat

PLANTING

PLANTING SEASON:	Spring
LIGHT REQUIREMENTS:	Full sun
HARDINESS ZONES:	7 to 10
SPACING:	4 feet (1.2 m)
HEIGHT:	7 to 8 feet (2.1 to 2.4 m)
WIDTH:	4 feet (1.2 m)
DISEASE RESISTANCE:	Excellent
CONTAINER PLANTING:	No

STRIPED ROSES ARE LIKE THUMBPRINTS: Every single one is unique. Bred by Delbard in France in 1999, Red Intuition is a red-striped variety with hues ranging from cherry red to a deep oxblood. This rose will lighten to more of a raspberry pink in high heat and turn a deep red in the cooler weather of spring and fall.

The blooms are borne on single stems and the plant will grow to 4 to 5 feet (1.2 to 1.5 m) tall. It is almost thornless, which is ideal for florists and a plus for gardens with children and pets running around.

This scarlet beauty is very vigorous and disease resistant, and with its long stems, it's a perfect cut flower. The stripes on Red Intuition are truly unexpected, making this a memorable choice for a garden with space for this stunning hybrid tea.

BASICS

ROSE TYPE:	Hybrid tea
BREEDER:	Guy Delbard
COLOR:	Red
FRAGRANCE:	Mild
BLOOM FORM:	High-centered
PETAL COUNT:	40
GROWTH TYPE:	Shrub
BLOOM TIME:	Repeat

PLANTING

PLANTING SEASON:	Spring
LIGHT REQUIREMENTS:	Full sun
HARDINESS ZONES:	7 to 10
SPACING:	4 feet (1.2 m)
HEIGHT:	4 to 5 feet (1.2 to 1.5 m)
WIDTH:	3 feet (0.9 m)
DISEASE RESISTANCE:	Excellent
CONTAINER PLANTING:	No

· DARK NIGHT ·

WHEN SEEN IN A FIELD OF ROSES, DARK Night is distinctive, thanks to its velvety-rich, deep red wine hues. There's no other rose in our garden quite like it, and it doesn't lose its striking dark color during the warm months like so many other red roses do.

This hybrid tea has lush, glossy, dark green foliage and large flowers with a very light fragrance. Another masterpiece in the Meilland line of roses, Dark Night is a prolific bloomer throughout the season. In coastal climates it does have the tendency to be susceptible to powdery mildew (for prevention tips, see page 247).

Dark Night is utterly romantic, and its super-soft petals truly resemble velvet, opening to reveal contrasting golden stamens. Living in Southern California, we often receive requests for this variety to accompany University of Southern California Trojans events and get-togethers. It's the perfect rose for any USC fan, as its deep burgundy hue and golden center look very close to the school's colors.

BASICS

ROSE TYPE:	Hybrid tea
BREEDER:	Meilland
COLOR:	Dark red, light yellow reverse
FRAGRANCE:	Mild
BLOOM FORM:	High-centered
PETAL COUNT:	27
GROWTH TYPE:	Bushy
BLOOM TIME:	Repeat

PLANTING

PLANTING SEASON:	Spring
LIGHT REQUIREMENTS:	Full sun
HARDINESS ZONES:	5 to 10
SPACING:	4 feet (1.2 m)
HEIGHT:	4 to 6 feet (1.2 to 1.8 m)
WIDTH:	3 to 4 feet (0.9 to 1.2 m)
DISEASE RESISTANCE:	Good
CONTAINER PLANTING:	No

CREAM
and
WHITE

· BOLERO ·

BOLERO IS ONE OF MY FAVORITES: spectacular in the garden and a stunner in the vase. For a white rose, it's as carefree as they come in terms of maintenance and growth, resulting in large, generous sprays from spring through fall. This romantic rose has a heavenly sweet perfume reminiscent of fruity candy, with subtle hints of tea. It makes a beautiful addition to any garden, especially for those who love the old-world charm and the romance of ruffled white roses.

Almost completely disease-free in most climates and prolific when given lots of sun, Bolero is truly one of the best white garden roses to grow and design with. It blooms on straight, upright, and moderately thorny stems adorned with either massive single blossoms or clusters of five to seven flowers.

This rose is on the smaller side, so it's a good choice for front-of-the-garden placement. Plants can be grown close together to form a hedgerow, but keep in mind that Bolero needs full sun to thrive so choose the warmest spot in the garden and keep it free from moisture. This rose prefers dry climates more than other roses because of its petal density. Its blooms will ball in cool, damp climates. Bolero, even here in warm Southern California, maxes out at about 4 feet (1.2 m) tall and 3 feet (0.9 m) wide. In the spring and fall, the centers of this rose are blush and fade to pure white. In the warmer months, Bolero is pure white.

BASICS

ROSE TYPE:	Floribunda
BREEDER:	Jacques Mouchotte
COLOR:	White
FRAGRANCE:	Strong
BLOOM FORM:	Old-fashioned
PETAL COUNT:	150
GROWTH TYPE:	Upright, shrub
BLOOM TIME:	Repeat

PLANTING

PLANTING SEASON:	Spring
LIGHT REQUIREMENTS:	Full sun
HARDINESS ZONES:	5 to 9
SPACING:	3 feet (0.9 m)
HEIGHT:	3 to 4 feet (0.9 to 1.2 m)
WIDTH:	2 to 3 feet (0.6 to 0.9 m)
DISEASE RESISTANCE:	Excellent
CONTAINER PLANTING:	No

ICEBERG IS EASILY DISMISSED AS JUST A standard landscaping rose. But there is a reason for its ubiquity: Iceberg is one of the most hardy, vigorous, low-maintenance, disease-free roses ever bred. It is actually a vintage rose, full of sweet, whimsical charm, so don't be so quick to discount it. While Iceberg might not be the most fragrant rose or offer the most sought-after old-world form, it is both beautiful and attainable for all to grow. It flowers often throughout the season and is a real workhorse in the garden.

Iceberg produces large clusters of spray roses with gently overlapping petals. They make for beautiful cut flowers, with whimsical, fluttery, pure white blooms and beautiful golden stamens. If you cut a spray, just one or two stems will fill an entire vase.

There are versions of Iceberg that climb, but at our previous farm we lined the driveway with Iceberg shrubs. The plants were covered in blooms beginning in the spring and throughout the fall. Everyone who visited our farms remarked on the breathtaking entranceway.

BASICS

ROSE TYPE:	Hybrid tea
BREEDER:	Tim Hermann Kordes
COLOR:	White
FRAGRANCE:	Mild
BLOOM FORM:	Cupped
PETAL COUNT:	35 to 40
GROWTH TYPE:	Bushy, upright
BLOOM TIME:	Repeat

PLANTING

PLANTING SEASON:	Spring
LIGHT REQUIREMENTS:	Full sun
HARDINESS ZONES:	6 to 9
SPACING:	4 feet (1.2 m)
HEIGHT:	4 feet (1.2 m)
WIDTH:	3 feet (0.9 m)
DISEASE RESISTANCE:	Excellent
CONTAINER PLANTING:	No

· SALLY HOLMES ·

THERE IS NOTHING QUITE LIKE SALLY
Holmes, a dramatic, celebrated rose that I
lovingly call a "house eater" to capture the
magnitude with which it can grow and climb.
In our warm climate, this vigorous rose is a
behemoth. Sally Holmes is almost always in
bloom, and it is a magnificent climber. It grows
long stems that have free-flowing, single-
petaled flowers all the way down them.

In the springtime, the buds start out
looking like tiny peach scrolls, and they take
their time to open. Once they do, they reveal
massive, single-petal white blooms with bright
yellow stamens. As a border, hedge, archway,
and ornamental rose there is nothing that
compares to this variety. Sally Holmes's blooms
are 3 to 4 inches (8 to 10 cm), blossoming all
the way down the stem in big clusters. This
rose loves heat—the hotter it is, the more it
flowers. It requires a lot of deadheading because
it grows so prolifically, especially in the spring.
The good news is that as soon as you deadhead,
it comes right back into bloom.

BASICS

ROSE TYPE:	Climbing
BREEDER:	Robert A. Holmes
COLOR:	Cream, with yellow stamens
FRAGRANCE:	Mild
BLOOM FORM:	Single
PETAL COUNT:	5
GROWTH TYPE:	Climbing
BLOOM TIME:	Repeat

PLANTING

PLANTING SEASON:	Spring
LIGHT REQUIREMENTS:	Full sun
HARDINESS ZONES:	5 to 9
SPACING:	4 feet (1.2 m)
HEIGHT:	6 to 12 feet (1.8 to 3.7 m)
WIDTH:	3 to 5 feet (0.9 to 1.5 m)
DISEASE RESISTANCE:	Excellent
CONTAINER PLANTING:	No

· ALABASTER ·

A BEAUTIFUL WHITE FLORIBUNDA ROSE
bred by Tantau, Alabaster has won a Society of
American Florists Red Ribbon Award, and it's
easy to see why: This variety has a pale lemon-
yellow center that opens to pure white on the
petals, making it a great choice for gardeners
who want a white rose that isn't just a flat white
blossom.

Borne in clusters or on single stems, the
flowers on Alabaster are on the smaller side,
but they fully open until they become flat
rosettes. The cluster formation on the plant
results in an abundance of small, lovely blooms
on each bush.

Alabaster has a hefty ten-day vase life, so
its light and crisp flowers can be enjoyed for
longer than many other varieties. The glossy,
dark green foliage on the plant is an appealing
contrast to the rose's lemony tint, giving it
dimension in the garden.

BASICS

ROSE TYPE:	Floribunda
BREEDER:	Tantau
COLOR:	White
FRAGRANCE:	Light
BLOOM FORM:	Rosette
PETAL COUNT:	75
GROWTH TYPE:	Upright
BLOOM TIME:	Repeat

PLANTING

PLANTING SEASON:	Spring
LIGHT REQUIREMENTS:	Full sun
HARDINESS ZONES:	5 to 10
SPACING:	3 feet (0.9 m)
HEIGHT:	3 to 4 feet (0.9 to 1.2 m)
WIDTH:	2 to 3 feet (0.6 to 0.9 m)
DISEASE RESISTANCE:	Excellent
CONTAINER PLANTING:	No

EARTH ANGEL LOOKS A LOT LIKE
Kordes's Pompon Veranda (page 168) because
of its globular blooms with white outer petals
and blush-pink centers—but this variety is a
full-sized plant. A floribunda rose, Earth Angel
is peony-shaped, with a cupped bloom and large
sprays.

Earth Angel is beloved by many and a part
of Kordes's Parfuma collection, meaning it is
bred to be very fragrant. Hints of citrus and
sparkles of Champagne round out this fruit-
forward scent. Zoned for 5 to 10, this upright
rose is said to grow to 3 by 3 feet (0.9 to 0.9 m),
though my Earth Angel plants measure 4 by
4 feet (1.2 by 1.2 m). The substantial blooms
will appear more blush in cooler weather and
whiter in the fall, possibly balling up a bit in
moist climates.

BASICS

ROSE TYPE:	Floribunda
BREEDER:	Kordes
COLOR:	Cream pink
FRAGRANCE:	Strong
BLOOM FORM:	Globular, old-fashioned
PETAL COUNT:	90-plus
GROWTH TYPE:	Upright, bushy
BLOOM TIME:	Repeat

PLANTING

PLANTING SEASON:	Spring
LIGHT REQUIREMENTS:	Full sun
HARDINESS ZONES:	5 to 10
SPACING:	3 feet (0.9 m)
HEIGHT:	4 feet (1.2 m)
WIDTH:	3 feet (0.9 m)
DISEASE RESISTANCE:	Good
CONTAINER PLANTING:	No

I'LL NEVER FORGET THE FIRST TIME I walked past a blooming Clouds of Glory bush; it cemented my love of this variety. My husband, Ryan, and I had just purchased our first home and we were busy preparing the garden. I was making sure everything was arranged properly before we started planting, and the aroma of this young bush still in its pot immediately caught my attention. I became energized and excited about the potential for our new backyard and what this rose, as well as the others, would produce.

It's not just the fragrance that makes this variety stand out but also its large ruffled blooms. The nearly thornless stems are long with hunter-green foliage that beautifully contrasts with the white petals. The flowers appear on single stems as well as in huge sprays. They're white with hints of blush that tend to fade as the roses open. It's easy to see how Clouds of Glory got its name—when the blossoms are fully open, they resemble puffy clouds in the sky. A handful of cut stems will easily fill a vase without your needing to add other flowers.

Unlike many hybrid teas, Clouds of Glory fills in nicely with a bushy appearance. From above, its magnificent spring flush would make you believe you're looking at a fluffy blanket lying in the garden.

Of the hundreds of varieties of roses we currently grow on our farm, Clouds of Glory is one of only two that we keep purely for pleasure. While it makes a perfect cut flower, we don't ship Clouds of Glory to our clients because the large, ruffled petals bruise easily during transit. However, this rose's undeniable beauty gives it a permanent spot on our farm.

BASICS

ROSE TYPE:	Hybrid tea
BREEDER:	Jackson & Perkins
COLOR:	White
FRAGRANCE:	Strong
BLOOM FORM:	High-centered
PETAL COUNT:	40-plus
GROWTH TYPE:	Upright, shrub
BLOOM TIME:	Repeat

PLANTING

PLANTING SEASON:	Spring
LIGHT REQUIREMENTS:	Full sun
HARDINESS ZONES:	5 to 10
SPACING:	4 feet (1.2 m)
HEIGHT:	Up to 6 feet (1.8 m)
WIDTH:	4 feet (1.2 m)
DISEASE RESISTANCE:	Excellent
CONTAINER PLANTING:	No

• LICHFIELD ANGEL •

DAVID AUSTIN'S LICHFIELD ANGEL, OUR favorite cream rose, is one of the most fascinating to watch as it unfurls. The bloom slowly opens in stages beginning with the pale peachy pink bud, which forms a perfectly rounded ball shape. As it opens, the inner petals appear as a stunning cupped rosette. Once the bloom reaches its full glory the large, ruffled petals create a magnificent dome.

In our production field, Lichfield Angel gets off to a slow start each spring. However, once the flowers start appearing, it's an excellent repeater throughout the season. The nearly thornless stems can be straight or wispy, with elegantly nodding blooms. With its consistent cream coloring and its very mild musk fragrance, Lichfield Angel is a great addition to most arrangements, no matter the season.

As a shrub rose with semi-glossy green foliage, it makes an excellent hedge or border in a garden setting. Lichfield Angel, like many of David Austin's roses, is very disease resistant and grows well in most climates.

BASICS

ROSE TYPE:	English shrub
BREEDER:	David Austin
COLOR:	Cream
FRAGRANCE:	Light
BLOOM FORM:	Cupped, rosette
PETAL COUNT:	100
GROWTH TYPE:	Medium shrub
BLOOM TIME:	Repeat

PLANTING

PLANTING SEASON:	Spring
LIGHT REQUIREMENTS:	Full sun
HARDINESS ZONES:	5 to 9
SPACING:	4 feet (1.2 m)
HEIGHT:	4 feet (1.2 m)
WIDTH:	4 feet (1.2 m)
DISEASE RESISTANCE:	Excellent
CONTAINER PLANTING:	No

· TRANQUILLITY ·

TRANQUILLITY IS A PURE WHITE
English rose from David Austin. It blooms
prolifically in spring and continues reliably
throughout the fall. Tranquillity's scent is
on the mild side for an English rose and can
best be described as clean and fresh; I liken it
to the aroma of clean laundry with a dash of
citrus. For those who prefer a more delicate
rose fragrance, the subtlety of Tranquillity is
perfect.

Young plants will produce flowers the first
year, but they improve with age; after a few
seasons, the plants throw long, beautifully
arching canes covered in stems and flowers.
Tranquillity's blooms are sturdy and almost
never bruise, a true miracle for a white rose.
Most stems are sprays with one large terminal
bud and side buds around. The buds have a
red tinge at the tips but turn pure white when
fully open. This variety has glossy, bright
green leaves borne on straight, sturdy stems.
Tranquillity's foliage is some of the cleanest,
most disease-free we grow.

A low-maintenance and robust bloomer,
Tranquillity tends to grow quite large, so give
the plants adequate space. In warmer climates
they will climb beautifully up a short arbor or
trellis.

BASICS

ROSE TYPE:	English shrub
BREEDER:	David Austin
COLOR:	White
FRAGRANCE:	Mild
BLOOM FORM:	Rosette
PETAL COUNT:	110
GROWTH TYPE:	Medium shrub
BLOOM TIME:	Repeat

PLANTING

PLANTING SEASON:	Spring
LIGHT REQUIREMENTS:	Full sun
HARDINESS ZONES:	5 to 9
SPACING:	4 feet (1.2 m)
HEIGHT:	4 feet (1.2 m)
WIDTH:	4 feet (1.2 m)
DISEASE RESISTANCE:	Excellent
CONTAINER PLANTING:	No

· POMPON VERANDA ·

POMPON VERANDA FEATURES ADORABLE globular blooms with white outer petals and the sweetest pink centers. This rose was bred by Kordes in 2007 and grows to be about 2 to 3 feet (0.6 to 0.9 m) wide, making it manageable and well suited for a container.

This precious rose grows in massive sprays, but the bloom itself is only 1.5 to 2 inches (4 to 5 cm) wide. However, because the flowers grow in clusters, they have a lot of impact. Many globular roses will ball up in moist weather, but Pompon Veranda will not. It is zoned 5 to 9, will repeat, and is disease resistant.

These ruffled spherical blossoms are as darling as can be and, with their light fragrance, are sure to bring a smile to anyone passing by in the garden.

BASICS

ROSE TYPE:	Floribunda
BREEDER:	Kordes
COLOR:	Cream pink
FRAGRANCE:	Mild
BLOOM FORM:	Globular, cupped
PETAL COUNT:	50-plus
GROWTH TYPE:	Bushy
BLOOM TIME:	Repeat

PLANTING

PLANTING SEASON:	Spring
LIGHT REQUIREMENTS:	Full sun
HARDINESS ZONES:	5 to 9
SPACING:	3 feet (0.9 m)
HEIGHT:	2 to 3 feet (0.6 to 0.9 m)
WIDTH:	2 to 3 feet (0.6 to 0.9 m)
DISEASE RESISTANCE:	Excellent
CONTAINER PLANTING:	Yes

WHEN I FIRST SAW THIS ROSE, I WAS visiting a nursery and walked by many pots of Shirley's Bouquet and thought to myself, "These are pretty, maybe I'll buy some." As I bent down to smell the rose, I was completely taken aback by its deep, heady fragrance.

The next thing I noticed was the thickness of pure white, creamy petals on the flower. Many white roses bruise easily—in the rain or especially when you ship them—but the substantial petals on this rose hardly ever do. Shirley's Bouquet blooms nonstop, and once you harvest, a cut flower will last for a week in a vase.

Since that day at the nursery, Shirley's Bouquet has become a staple at our farm. We grow two thousand of these plants, a true testament to their hardiness and beauty.

BASICS

ROSE TYPE:	Hybrid tea
BREEDER:	Pierre Orard
COLOR:	White
FRAGRANCE:	Strong
BLOOM FORM:	High-centered
PETAL COUNT:	25 to 35
GROWTH TYPE:	Upright, bushy
BLOOM TIME:	Repeat

PLANTING

PLANTING SEASON:	Spring
LIGHT REQUIREMENTS:	Full sun
HARDINESS ZONES:	5 to 9
SPACING:	3 to 4 feet (0.9 to 1.2 m)
HEIGHT:	3 to 4 feet (0.9 to 1.2 m)
WIDTH:	3 to 4 feet (0.9 to 1.2 m)
DISEASE RESISTANCE:	Excellent
CONTAINER PLANTING:	No

· POPE JOHN PAUL II ·

IT IS EXTREMELY RARE FOR US TO GROW a rose that we don't offer as a cut flower. But for Pope John Paul II we make an exception—the petals are too fragile for shipping, but this is one of my favorite garden roses. We first started growing this variety in our garden about six years ago, and have planted more than two hundred bushes in our front yard as landscaping. Pope John Paul II is such a show-off rose, with massive, ruffled, layered blooms and nearly perfect breeding.

To know this rose is to love it! It is a true white, with no cream or yellow undertones, and its perfectly rounded buds open to reveal ruffled, enormous garden roses. Roses are borne on single stems as well as in clusters. The foliage is dark and matte, which is a striking contrast to the pure white blooms. The stems have almost no thorns—a true miracle.

Walking through a field of Pope John Paul II is reminiscent of being in a citrus grove. If you close your eyes, you'll forget that you are sniffing a rose. The sweet, hard-to-describe, almost lemony fragrance is so bright and unique.

The plants are very generous bloomers, disease resistant, and they form nicely rounded shrubs. If you plant them 2 to 3 feet (0.6 to 0.9 m) apart, they'll form a beautiful hedge. Just as a bloom cycle is complete, the plant is already putting up new buds. While we don't cut these for our business, the "Pope" will always have a home on our farm.

BASICS

ROSE TYPE:	Hybrid tea
BREEDER:	Dr. Keith W. Zary
COLOR:	White
FRAGRANCE:	Strong
BLOOM FORM:	High-centered
PETAL COUNT:	30
GROWTH TYPE:	Upright, shrub
BLOOM TIME:	Repeat

PLANTING

PLANTING SEASON:	Spring
LIGHT REQUIREMENTS:	Full sun
HARDINESS ZONES:	6 to 9
SPACING:	4 feet (1.2 m)
HEIGHT:	5 feet (1.5 m)
WIDTH:	3 feet (0.9 m)
DISEASE RESISTANCE:	Excellent
CONTAINER PLANTING:	No

WHEN WE STARTED OUR BUSINESS IN 2016, I bought out the entire inventory of French Lace from Otto and Sons after seeing it in a catalog. This rose's precious, antique feel stands out among cream roses. Its spring blooms, when fully open, are cream with peach undertones. In the summer the flowers will be more cream-toned with white centers.

When French Lace's blossoms are mature, the petals almost roll back, and the faces appear flat, resulting in a plush, robust flower that adds a softness to the garden. While the name French Lace implies it is delicate, this rose is quite the opposite when it comes to hardiness. It holds up well to cutting and shipping and lasts long in a vase. Its durability makes it a perfect wedding bouquet rose.

If you're willing to handle its thorny stems you'll be rewarded, as French Lace is very disease resistant and one of the prettiest cream-to-white roses I've grown.

BASICS

ROSE TYPE:	Floribunda
BREEDER:	Warriner
COLOR:	Apricot to peach
FRAGRANCE:	Light
BLOOM FORM:	High-centered
PETAL COUNT:	35
GROWTH TYPE:	Small shrub
BLOOM TIME:	Repeat

PLANTING

PLANTING SEASON:	Spring
LIGHT REQUIREMENTS:	Full sun
HARDINESS ZONES:	6 to 11
SPACING:	4 feet (1.2 m)
HEIGHT:	3 feet (0.9 m)
WIDTH:	2 feet (0.6 m)
DISEASE RESISTANCE:	Excellent
CONTAINER PLANTING:	No

· WHITE EDEN ·

OCCASIONALLY, A BREEDER WILL INTEND for a rose to be a particular color, but a genetic mutation will occur, causing the rose to take on a different look. This mutation is called a sport, and it can result in a plant being a different color or perhaps having a different blooming pattern than the breed had reliably shown in the past. White Eden is a white sport of Eden (page 73), which is typically a very punchy pink rose.

Eden is known and treasured for its vigor, heavy blooms, romantic shape, and fragrance—and White Eden possesses all those qualities in a new palette. This variety is a gateway to becoming a rose lover as it is an accessible climber that is disease resistant and provides an enchanting sight with its repeat blooms. This plant is always covered in flowers, and its cupped blossoms are breathtaking to behold. When the roses meet full maturity, they open all the way.

Ideal for Zones 5 to 10, this creamy white rose with its contrasting green foliage and delicious light fragrance would do well in a garden with enough space to let it shine.

BASICS

ROSE TYPE:	Climbing
BREEDER:	Meilland
COLOR:	Creamy white
FRAGRANCE:	Light
BLOOM FORM:	Old-fashioned, globular
PETAL COUNT:	100 to 110
GROWTH TYPE:	Climbing
BLOOM TIME:	Repeat

PLANTING

PLANTING SEASON:	Spring
LIGHT REQUIREMENTS:	Full sun
HARDINESS ZONES:	5 to 10
SPACING:	3 to 4 feet (0.9 to 1.2 m)
HEIGHT:	10 to 12 feet (3 to 3.7 m)
WIDTH:	4 feet (1.2 m)
DISEASE RESISTANCE:	Good
CONTAINER PLANTING:	No

AN HEIRLOOM CLIMBER, SOMBREUIL WAS bred in 1850 and is still in circulation—and unlike many rarer heirloom roses, this variety is readily found in nurseries and garden centers.

Sombreuil flaunts an intense old-rose fragrance and can grow to be a very large plant with magnificent splendor. Multiple Sombreuil plants will cover a wall effectively or climb handsomely over a fence, arbor, arch, or anything on which they can attach themselves.

The bloom features four quadrants in the center that radiate out, with a large terminal flower in the middle and sweet side buds. This creamy quartered blossom is fully flat when open and has a Champagne tinge. Hardy in Zones 6 to 11, Sombreuil makes a good cut flower, and the plant is resplendent with staggering roses in the springtime.

BASICS

ROSE TYPE:	Climbing
BREEDER:	Unknown
COLOR:	White
FRAGRANCE:	Medium to strong
BLOOM FORM:	Quartered, rosette
PETAL COUNT:	25
GROWTH TYPE:	Climbing
BLOOM TIME:	Repeat

PLANTING

PLANTING SEASON:	Spring
LIGHT REQUIREMENTS:	Full
HARDINESS ZONES:	6 to 11
SPACING:	4 to 6 feet (1.2 to 1.8 m)
HEIGHT:	15 feet (4.6 m)
WIDTH:	3 to 4 feet (0.9 to 1.2 m)
DISEASE RESISTANCE:	Good
CONTAINER PLANTING:	No

THIS VARIETY WAS BRED BY KORDES IN Germany and is a vigorous, healthy climber that could be described as the modern version of Sombreuil (opposite). Honeymoon blooms are an elegant, creamy white that can have a hint of blush in warmer weather. This rose is readily available in nurseries, disease resistant, and accessible to people in cooler and warmer climates alike, with an old-fashioned rose fragrance.

Honeymoon is an easy-to-care-for climber, ideal for beginners or gardeners who have never worked with a climbing rose before. It fills that longing to have a picturesque walkway with romantic roses weaving up and through an arch—that perfect fairy-tale look—without requiring a lot of maintenance.

BASICS

ROSE TYPE:	Climbing
BREEDER:	Kordes
COLOR:	White
FRAGRANCE:	Mild
BLOOM FORM:	Cupped
PETAL COUNT:	50
GROWTH TYPE:	Climbing
BLOOM TIME:	Repeat

PLANTING

PLANTING SEASON:	Spring
LIGHT REQUIREMENTS:	Full sun
HARDINESS ZONES:	5 to 9
SPACING:	4 to 5 feet (1.2 to 1.5 m)
HEIGHT:	7 feet (2.1 m)
WIDTH:	4 feet (1.2 m)
DISEASE RESISTANCE:	Excellent
CONTAINER PLANTING:	No

ONE OF THE MOST RELIABLE ROSES THAT we grow, Pure Perfume also happens to be one of the most unassuming plants in our production field. It is not one of those roses that will pull you in as you stroll through our garden. Don't let that dissuade you, though: This rose is an incredible beauty. What it lacks in showiness it makes up for with form and fragrance: lush foliage, an unforgettable citrus scent, and crisp white cup-shaped buds that open fully to flat rosettes that resemble stars perched upon semi-thornless stems. From the first spring flush until the winter prune, Pure Perfume is never short on stems to cut.

This shrub rose from breeder Jackson & Perkins has become the predominant white rose that we grow at Grace Rose Farm. The pure-white petals are incredibly hardy and hold up well during cross-country shipment. The roses grow as single-bloom stems and in magnificent clusters. The fully open flower complements other flowers in an arrangement while looking equally stunning in a vase by itself.

I often keep a vase full of Pure Perfume in my kitchen and find that its citrusy scent helps me start my day on the right note. This rose is a daily reminder that there is beauty in simplicity.

BASICS

ROSE TYPE:	Shrub
BREEDER:	Dr. Keith W. Zary
COLOR:	White
FRAGRANCE:	Strong
BLOOM FORM:	Cupped
PETAL COUNT:	41
GROWTH TYPE:	Shrub, sprawling
BLOOM TIME:	Repeat

PLANTING

PLANTING SEASON:	Spring
LIGHT REQUIREMENTS:	Full sun
HARDINESS ZONES:	6 to 9
SPACING:	4 feet (1.2 m)
HEIGHT:	5 feet (1.5 m)
WIDTH:	5 feet (1.5 m)
DISEASE RESISTANCE:	Excellent
CONTAINER PLANTING:	No

YELLOW

WE HAVE BEEN GROWING BUTTERSCOTCH as a cut rose since we started our farm in 2016. This rose is not widely commercially available, but if you are able to find it to plant, it is an extremely vigorous, unusual-colored rose. The blooms start out a mustard hue, but when fully blown out in the sun, they become the most beautiful shade of sepia tan. If you bring the flowers inside before they blow out, you'll get more of a honey color. Florists love this rose for arranging because, as a climber, it has very flexible stems. But as the plant grows laterally, the stems are atypically short—just 8 to 10 inches (20 to 25 cm).

This variety is disease resistant, transplants well, and grows vigorously. The spring flush for this rose is the most prolific, showcasing blossoms in sprays on dark matte foliage. After the spring bloom, Butterscotch tends to flower only once more toward the fall season.

BASICS

ROSE TYPE:	Climbing
BREEDER:	William A. Warriner
COLOR:	Tan
FRAGRANCE:	Mild
BLOOM FORM:	High-centered
PETAL COUNT:	25
GROWTH TYPE:	Climbing
BLOOM TIME:	Repeat

PLANTING

PLANTING SEASON:	Spring
LIGHT REQUIREMENTS:	Full sun
HARDINESS ZONES:	6 to 10
SPACING:	4 feet (1.2 m)
HEIGHT:	8 to 10 feet (2.4 to 3 m)
WIDTH:	4 (1.2 m)
DISEASE RESISTANCE:	Excellent
CONTAINER PLANTING:	No

· PEACE ·

ONE OF THE MOST BELOVED AND FAMOUS
roses of all time, Peace is a hybrid tea that
was bred by Meilland in France and named to
commemorate the end of World War II. It's the
second most grown rose in the United States
and has won numerous awards since its debut
in 1946. There are 350,000 plants produced
internationally of this adored variety, and many
roses have been bred from it, including Princess
Charlene de Monaco (page 61).

This is a classic, pointed-bud, double-
petaled hybrid tea with forty-five to fifty petals
per bloom. Those petals are a warm, golden
apricot hue that fades into a tipped blush edge,
an almost color-wash effect of sunset tones
cascading across each delicate petal. This rose
will grow to be over 6 feet (1.8 m) tall, and its
flowers are borne on single, straight, and sturdy
stems, making them ideal for cutting. The
fragrance is light and lovely, the perfect pairing
for one of the most celebrated roses in history.

BASICS

ROSE TYPE:	Hybrid tea
BREEDER:	Meilland
COLOR:	Yellow
FRAGRANCE:	Strong
BLOOM FORM:	Cupped
PETAL COUNT:	45 to 50
GROWTH TYPE:	Upright
BLOOM TIME:	Repeat

PLANTING

PLANTING SEASON:	Spring
LIGHT REQUIREMENTS:	Full sun
HARDINESS ZONES:	5 to 10
SPACING:	3 to 4 feet (0.9 to 1.2 m)
HEIGHT:	6 feet (1.8 m)
WIDTH:	3 feet (0.9 m)
DISEASE RESISTANCE:	Moderate
CONTAINER PLANTING:	No

· STEPHEN RULO ·

I FIRST CAME ACROSS THIS ROSE WHEN we started our journey in the cut rose industry many years ago. Stephen Rulo, for whom the rose was named, came to visit our farm and gave us permission to grow and multiply this variety. We now grow the largest collection of this rose in the world.

Bred from Honey Dijon (page 191) and Stainless Steel (page 129), Stephen Rulo has light lavender shading like Stainless Steel with warm, sunshine undertones reminiscent of Honey Dijon. As a result, the color on this rose is ethereal—and changeable. In the early spring when Honey Dijon and Stephen Rulo are both blooming next to each other in our field, you can't tell which is which except for the foliage (Honey Dijon is grass green; Stephen Rulo is darker). As the temperature gets warmer, the lavender and gray colors of Stainless Steel will come through in the petals of Stephen Rulo. In July, this rose will be quite lavender in color and can look very much like Stainless Steel. In the fall, when the weather cools down, the bloom goes back to a rich, sandy honey-toned shade.

Stephen Rulo is remarkably vigorous—if you stick a tiny root of this variety in the ground you will have a full rosebush six months later. It performs well in both warm and cool climates and is disease resistant thanks to its parent plants. Because of its thick, hardy stems that grow in massive sprays, this makes an excellent cut rose.

BASICS

ROSE TYPE:	Grandiflora
BREEDER:	William E. Chaney
COLOR:	Beige with gold base and lavender shading
FRAGRANCE:	Mild
BLOOM FORM:	High-centered
PETAL COUNT:	26 to 40
GROWTH TYPE:	Upright
BLOOM TIME:	Repeat

PLANTING

PLANTING SEASON:	Spring
LIGHT REQUIREMENTS:	Full sun
HARDINESS ZONES:	6 to 10
SPACING:	4 feet (1.2 m)
HEIGHT:	4 to 6 feet (1.2 to 1.8 m)
WIDTH:	2 to 3 feet (0.6 to 0.9 m)
DISEASE RESISTANCE:	Excellent
CONTAINER PLANTING:	No

THIS DAVID AUSTIN ENGLISH SHRUB ROSE is the most delightful shade of yellow, with paler outer petals that intensify to a buttery center. Its wilder look is reminiscent to me of vintage botanical artwork, an aesthetic that lends itself to a memorable impact in the garden.

While the delicate shading and tender petals of The Country Parson would suggest otherwise, this rose variety spans several zones, making it hardy for growing in many conditions.

The Country Parson has a medium, fruity fragrance and will bloom consistently from spring until the first frost.

BASICS

ROSE TYPE:	English shrub
BREEDER:	David Austin
COLOR:	Yellow
FRAGRANCE:	Medium
BLOOM FORM:	Rosette
PETAL COUNT:	95
GROWTH TYPE:	Shrub
BLOOM TIME:	Repeat

PLANTING

PLANTING SEASON:	Spring
LIGHT REQUIREMENTS:	Full sun
HARDINESS ZONES:	4 to 10
SPACING:	4 feet (1.2 m)
HEIGHT:	3 to 4 feet (0.9 to 1.2 m)
WIDTH:	3 to 4 feet (0.9 to 1.2 m)
DISEASE RESISTANCE:	Excellent
CONTAINER PLANTING:	No

THE GOLDEN-TO-APRICOT OMBRÉ PETALS on Fun in the Sun are what make this grandiflora rose so special. Bred by Christian Bédard at Weeks Roses, Fun in the Sun's blooms are borne in clusters, giving the plant an English-garden look. The dark apricot heart of its blossom flushes out into buttery yellow outer petals in a flower measuring 3 to 4 inches (8 to 10 cm) across, depending on how hot the weather is.

This rose bears a strong citrusy fragrance with a bit of spicy warmth to it, which is fitting for its cheerful and carefree coloring. Fun in the Sun is a wonderfully romantic and old-world-looking rose that will bring a dose of sunshine to the garden.

BASICS

ROSE TYPE:	Grandiflora
BREEDER:	Christian Bédard
COLOR:	Yellow
FRAGRANCE:	Strong
BLOOM FORM:	Rosette
PETAL COUNT:	85-plus
GROWTH TYPE:	Upright, bushy
BLOOM TIME:	Repeat

PLANTING

PLANTING SEASON:	Spring
LIGHT REQUIREMENTS:	Full sun
HARDINESS ZONES:	4 to 10
SPACING:	4 feet (1.2 m)
HEIGHT:	4 to 6 feet (1.2 to 1.8 m)
WIDTH:	3 to 4 feet (0.9 to 1.2 m)
DISEASE RESISTANCE:	Excellent
CONTAINER PLANTING:	No

GOLDEN–MUSTARD PETALS KISSED WITH hints of pink make this uniquely colored rose a standout in any arrangement. Immensely popular among florists for its subtle, neutral hues and ability to complement almost any other flower, Honey Dijon quickly became one of the most sought-after roses in our field.

Honey Dijon is a very special rose to us at Grace Rose Farm, and it took years of perseverance to grow our collection. This rose is in high demand with gardeners, and the desirability of Honey Dijon rosebushes ensures that they are often sold out at florists and nurseries. Some think this variety has an almost caramel-like fragrance, which so uniquely matches its beautiful golden coloring. Honey Dijon is especially striking when it is fully open.

BASICS

ROSE TYPE:	Grandiflora
BREEDER:	James A. Sproul
COLOR:	Tan
FRAGRANCE:	Mild to strong
BLOOM FORM:	High-centered
PETAL COUNT:	26 to 40
GROWTH TYPE:	Bushy, upright
BLOOM TIME:	Repeat

PLANTING

PLANTING SEASON:	Spring
LIGHT REQUIREMENTS:	Full sun
HARDINESS ZONES:	6 to 9
SPACING:	4 feet (1.2 m)
HEIGHT:	5 feet (1.5 m)
WIDTH:	2 to 3 feet (0.6 to 0.9 m)
DISEASE RESISTANCE:	Good
CONTAINER PLANTING:	No

· GOLDEN CELEBRATION ·

OUT OF THE HUNDREDS OF VARIETIES WE grow at Grace Rose Farm, we have only one true yellow rose, and that's Golden Celebration. This is not your ordinary yellow rose. It has rich golden-sepia petals with soft whispers of lighter sunshine hues. This David Austin masterpiece has won multiple awards and is well known for its enchanting fragrance, a layering of tea notes with delightful hints of fresh strawberry.

Golden Celebration is a very prolific bloomer and provides us with abundant stems from the beginning of spring until we prune for our winter dormancy period. It is a great cut flower, with long stems and an extended vase life of three to four days.

Like so many of David Austin's roses, Golden Celebration is very disease resistant and makes a wonderful shrub, hedge, or sprawling rosebush that stands out in any garden. The long, arching canes can grow to over 8 feet (2.4 m) in height or can be trained to climb. The foliage is dark green, and the large blooms are deep cups with layers of beautiful yellow petals.

BASICS

ROSE TYPE:	English shrub
BREEDER:	David Austin
COLOR:	Golden yellow
FRAGRANCE:	Strong
BLOOM FORM:	Cupped
PETAL COUNT:	55 to 75
GROWTH TYPE:	Shrub or short climber
BLOOM TIME:	Repeat

PLANTING

PLANTING SEASON:	Spring
LIGHT REQUIREMENTS:	Full sun
HARDINESS ZONES:	5 to 10
SPACING:	5 feet (1.5 m)
HEIGHT:	8 feet (2.4 m)
WIDTH:	5 feet (1.5 m)
DISEASE RESISTANCE:	Excellent
CONTAINER PLANTING:	No

· VANESSA BELL ·

VANESSA BELL IS A VERY FULL, ROBUST
plant that can easily be grown in either the
ground or a container. Bred by David Austin,
this English shrub rose has similar color and
shading to The Country Parson (page 188) but
features a beautiful, more cup-shaped bloom.
This variety has a very strong tea fragrance
and is more robust than it is citrusy.

Buttery, canary-yellow blooms cover this
plant, showcasing a dazzling display of the
almost translucent petals. I've had it planted
at my home for a year, and it's always in
flower, so we enjoy these sunshine blooms
regularly. This rose is suitable for Zones 5 to
11, making it a great option for many climates.
I recommend planting Vanessa Bell as a border
rose along a walkway so the roses can spill
over romantically as you walk by. With crisp
green foliage, Vanessa Bell will brighten up any
garden or patio where it is planted.

BASICS

ROSE TYPE:	English shrub
BREEDER:	David Austin
COLOR:	Pale yellow
FRAGRANCE:	Strong
BLOOM FORM:	Cupped
PETAL COUNT:	70-plus
GROWTH TYPE:	Shrub
BLOOM TIME:	Repeat

PLANTING

PLANTING SEASON:	Spring
LIGHT REQUIREMENTS:	Full sun
HARDINESS ZONES:	5 to 11
SPACING:	3 to 4 feet (0.9 to 1.2 m)
HEIGHT:	4 feet (1.2 m)
WIDTH:	3 feet (0.9 m)
DISEASE RESISTANCE:	Excellent
CONTAINER PLANTING:	Yes

LA PARK, A VERY UPRIGHT FLORIBUNDA
rose, was named in commemoration of Park
Seed Company's 150th anniversary. To see this
striped rose in person is to truly know and
appreciate the splendor of color that is spread
across its petals. With its unique apricot to
yellow to coral hues, every bloom and every
petal has its own watercolor markings. The
deep apricot heart fades and wanes, layer upon
layer, into a creamy, translucent shade on the
outer petals. The sight is truly mesmerizing.

La Park will bloom prolifically all season
long and leave a lasting, rich tea fragrance.

BASICS

ROSE TYPE:	Floribunda
BREEDER:	Jackson & Perkins
COLOR:	Peach, pink
FRAGRANCE:	Strong
BLOOM FORM:	Old-fashioned
PETAL COUNT:	25-plus
GROWTH TYPE:	Upright, bushy
BLOOM TIME:	Repeat

PLANTING

PLANTING SEASON:	Spring
LIGHT REQUIREMENTS:	Full sun
HARDINESS ZONES:	5 to 10
SPACING:	4 feet (1.2 m)
HEIGHT:	3 to 4 feet (0.9 to 1.2 m)
WIDTH:	3 to 4 feet (0.9 to 1.2 m)
DISEASE RESISTANCE:	Excellent
CONTAINER PLANTING:	No

· MOONLIGHT ROMANTICA ·

WITH ITS LEMONY, SWEET FRAGRANCE
and saturated sunny petals, Moonlight
Romantica is a rose with so much personality.
One of the Romantica roses bred in France by
Meilland, Moonlight Romantica is a vigorous
rose with perfectly golden-yellow cup-shaped
blooms. But back in 2016 when I started
growing this variety, I couldn't sell it for the
life of me, so I gave away my plants. No one was
interested in buying sunshine yellow. Now this
rose is back in high demand and our new farm
has 250 Moonlight Romantica roses planted in
the production field.

This hybrid tea has a rounded, bushy shape
with upright stems and will grow tall but stay
rather mannerly in width. It will also perform
well in Zones 5 to 9, so many areas can enjoy
its cheerful petals and deep glossy green
foliage.

BASICS

ROSE TYPE:	Hybrid tea
BREEDER:	Meilland
COLOR:	Yellow
FRAGRANCE:	Strong
BLOOM FORM:	Cupped
PETAL COUNT:	26 to 40
GROWTH TYPE:	Upright
BLOOM TIME:	Repeat

PLANTING

PLANTING SEASON:	Spring
LIGHT REQUIREMENTS:	Full sun
HARDINESS ZONES:	5 to 9
SPACING:	4 feet (1.2 m)
HEIGHT:	4 to 6 feet (1.2 to 1.8 m)
WIDTH:	3 to 4 feet (0.9 to 1.2 m)
DISEASE RESISTANCE:	Excellent
CONTAINER PLANTING:	No

THIS ROSE WAS ORIGINALLY CALLED THE Huntington 100 Rose, named after the Rose Garden at the Huntington Library in San Marino, California. Bred by my friend Christian Bédard at Weeks Roses, this variety has since been renamed Life of the Party but still features the same spectacular bright pink and yellow hues.

When I visited the Huntington's Rose Garden with my husband, I encountered Life of the Party planted en masse for the first time, and it took my breath away. I had never seen such a beautiful yellow spray rose with pink-tipped petals, and the number of blooms on this plant was impressive. Though this shrub is manageable at about 3.5 feet (1 m) wide, it is dripping with old-fashioned flowers, a yellow, citrusy hue shining out from its green foliage.

Along with the unbelievable beauty of its blooms, Life of the Party has one of the most delightful, delectable fragrances I've ever experienced. You just want to walk around with this bright, citrusy and fruity rose under your nose all day long. Life of the Party is the perfect name for this variety because it's so happy and radiant, and I'm proud to know the people who bred and named it.

BASICS

ROSE TYPE:	Shrub
BREEDER:	Christian Bédard
COLOR:	Yellow tipped with pink
FRAGRANCE:	Strong
BLOOM FORM:	Old-fashioned
PETAL COUNT:	55 to 65
GROWTH TYPE:	Shrub
BLOOM TIME:	Repeat

PLANTING

PLANTING SEASON:	Spring
LIGHT REQUIREMENTS:	Full sun
HARDINESS ZONES:	6 to 10
SPACING:	3 to 4 feet (0.9 to 1.2 m)
HEIGHT:	3 to 4 feet (0.9 to 1.2 m)
WIDTH:	3 feet (0.9 m)
DISEASE RESISTANCE:	Excellent
CONTAINER PLANTING:	No

Part Two

GROWING ROSES

CHAPTER THREE

The

BEST VARIETIES

for

EVERY

CLIMATE

I understand the excitement that can come over you when you've decided to grow roses. But well before you choose which roses to plant, and where and how to plant them, you need to identify the climate in which you live. More times than not, if a rose fails to bloom, it's because it was planted in an area that is not appropriate for the variety.

GET TO KNOW YOUR CLIMATE

THE UNITED STATES DEPARTMENT OF AGRICULTURE (USDA) created a Plant Hardiness Zone Map that outlines the thirteen different climate zones in the US and the temperature range that can occur in each one, which will tell you whether a certain plant will grow successfully in that climate.

When you buy a rosebush for planting, the seller will provide information on the zone(s) in which that variety will grow healthily, with the least intervention. In general, roses are happiest in a dry Mediterranean climate where the temperatures don't fluctuate much. In humid or subtropical climates, or wet climates where it rains a lot during the growing season, they are prone to disease. In colder climates rose growing is possible, but the season is much shorter. Roses can technically be grown in most of the US, but Alaska (Zones 1 and 2) and parts of southern Florida and Hawaii (Zones 11 to 13) offer climate extremes that make growing roses difficult.

Even with my prior rose experience, I once found out the hard way that I had not done my zone research, and it cost me many beautiful rose plants.

When we started our first farm in Southern California's Ventura County, we were farming in Zone 10. Zone 10 is essentially the perfect climate for growing roses because there are nice, moderate temperatures all year long and no signs of frost. So when my husband and I bought our next farm just 90 miles (145 km) away, we assumed we'd be moving to the same zone. In February 2018 we dug up about six thousand rosebushes and moved them to our new farm in Santa Barbara County. Within days, we got frost. I had *never* experienced frost in Southern California in four years of owning my business and farming here—and that's when it dawned on me that I hadn't checked the USDA Plant Hardiness Zone Map. When I finally did, I was shocked. We had moved from Zone 10b to a microclimate (see opposite), Zone 9a. I had transplanted roses that thrived in heat and never felt temperatures below 50°F (10°C) to a climate where it reached as low as 19°F (–7°C) in the morning. Many of the rosebushes we moved died or had cane dieback, which happens when the cane turns black from being too cold (see page 208 for more on preventing cane dieback).

My husband and I had thought, "California is California; it's beautiful everywhere." But we learned very quickly that paying attention to where you're gardening is crucial. Our 90-mile (145 km) move meant a world of difference in climate, and not realizing that in time cost us hundreds of rosebushes and a lot of effort trying to save the ones that struggled. I learned my own lesson the hard way: Always do your research.

Often, we might have our hearts set on a particular variety, but it may not thrive in our climate as well as a very similar variety can. Being open-minded when selecting roses will set you up for growing those that are best suited for your climate or microclimate. In the pages that follow, I'll offer growing tips and tried-and-true plant varieties for the most common USDA Plant Hardiness Zones.

GO LOCAL

IN ADDITION TO RESEARCHING WHAT ZONE YOU LIVE IN BY looking at the USDA Plant Hardiness Zone Map (or the plant hardiness zone map in your country, if outside the US), the best thing you can do to find out which roses will grow most successfully in your area is to talk to local growers. Find a locally owned and operated garden center or nursery (not a big box or corporate home improvement store) and see what plants they're selling. A local garden center in Michigan isn't going to sell all the roses that I grow in California because many of them won't be suited for that climate. The people working at these businesses will be knowledgeable about what plants grow well in your specific environment and climate.

You might also want to attend a meeting of the nearest rose society; these local rosarians can tell you which rose varieties will thrive where you live (in the US, you can visit rose.org to find the nearest American Rose Society branch in your area).

MIND YOUR MICROCLIMATES

A microclimate is a small area where the climate differs or swings greatly from its surrounding region. Microclimates can see differences in temperature of multiple degrees or substantial shifts in humidity from that in an area just 3 miles (5 km) away. Make sure to find out if you live in a microclimate by talking to your local garden club (see above). Understanding your proximity to a microclimate makes a big difference in the kind of plants and roses you can successfully grow.

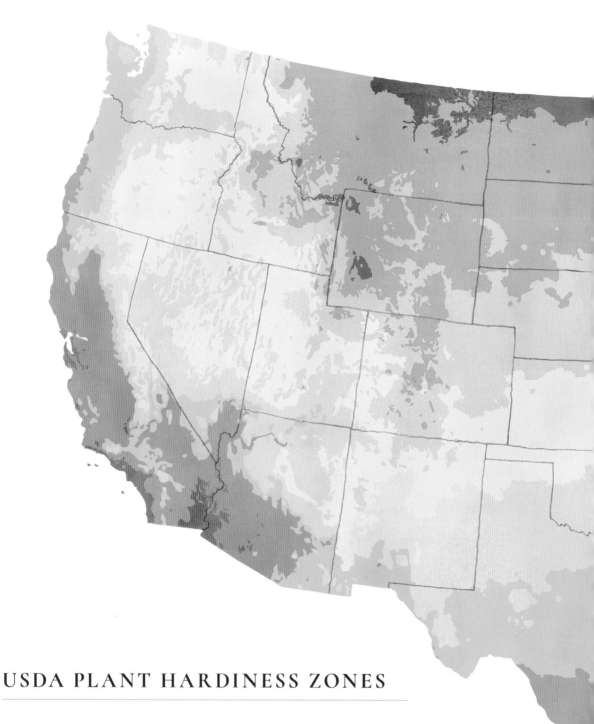

USDA PLANT HARDINESS ZONES

THE USDA PLANT HARDINESS ZONES DIFFER GREATLY, AS
temperatures and climates shift from zone to zone; rose care will vary
accordingly. The following pages offer some helpful tips to employ in each of
these zones to ensure your roses will be poised for success in your garden.

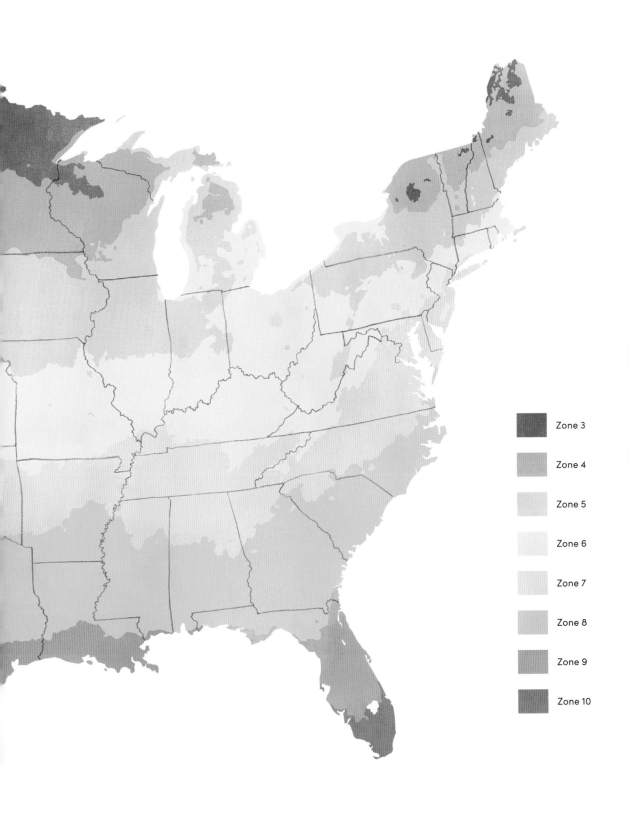

Zone 3

Zone 4

Zone 5

Zone 6

Zone 7

Zone 8

Zone 9

Zone 10

GROWING TIPS

Zones 3 and 4 are on the chilly side for roses, so extra care needs to be put into keeping them warm.

- Plant roses in raised beds, where the soil will be more quickly warmed by the sun than it would in the ground.

- Grow own-root rather than grafted roses (more on this on page 231). When planted in these zones, grafted rosebushes tend to rot off at the graft or die back completely in their first test season, leaving only the hardy rootstock.

- Use mulch or other frost protection to keep roses safe in the winter, especially those that have been planted for less than two years. Doing so will help prevent cane dieback, which occurs when the climate is cold enough that the exposed bare canes of the rosebush turn black and die. If your plant does experience cane dieback, trim the cane an inch (2.5 cm) below the damage and leave the healthy part intact. If the plant has dieback all the way to the soil, cut the entire cane out.

TRIED-AND-TRUE VARIETIES

Heritage

New Dawn (page 113)

Prairie Star

Quietness

Serendipity

New Dawn

GROWING TIPS

Zones 5 and 6, while not the coldest, will require diligent care to see successful bloom cycles. Staying on top of regular winter preparation and spring pruning and deadheading will ensure you make the most out of your growing season.

- Regularly deadhead your roses to encourage them to bloom again. Zones 5 and 6 experience short growing seasons, so this will provide your garden with the most roses given your zone.

- Shop for winter-hardy roses to prevent severe dieback; use winter protection on young roses (see page 232).

- Prune your roses around the time forsythia begin to bloom in late March, or when green stems start sprouting from the ground.

TRIED-AND-TRUE VARIETIES

Bolero (page 154)

Darcey Bussell (page 122)

Golden Celebration (page 192)

Princess Alexandra of Kent (page 97)

Summer Romance (page 83)

Golden Celebration

GROWING TIPS

Consistent disease prevention is key in Zones 7 and 8 to prevent your plants from experiencing blackspot and other fungal-related issues that go hand in hand with moister, more humid climates.

- Prune your roses around March 1 if you aren't expecting another frost.

- Keep up on spraying organic fungicides (see page 248) if you're in a moist climate to prevent blackspot.

TRIED-AND-TRUE VARIETIES

Bliss Parfuma (page 51)

Distant Drums (page 84)

Ebb Tide (page 124)

Marc Chagall (page 99)

The Lady Gardener (page 94)

The Lady Gardener

GROWING TIPS

Zones 9 and 10 enjoy very long growing seasons, but that typically comes with dry summers. A good watering routine is essential to keep your roses blooming throughout the season.

- Install drip irrigation: Your climate is most likely dry and warm with little rain in the growing season.

- Because of the long growing season, a summer pruning is sometimes necessary to tame roses. Gently cut back any overgrown top-growth (see page 254).

- If your garden is coastal, check your roses in the spring for powdery mildew and treat accordingly (see page 247).

TRIED-AND-TRUE VARIETIES

Francis Meilland (page 69)

Koko Loko (page 130)

Moonlight in Paris (page 76)

Traviata (page 141)

Yves Piaget (page 107)

Moonlight in Paris

CHAPTER FOUR

PLANNING

a

ROSE GARDEN

Perhaps you're visiting a botanical garden or someone's home with an inspiring garden and the property is resplendent with the most magnificent roses, their scent a delightful and cheery gift that stays with you even in memory. You think to yourself, "If only I could bottle up this moment and take it home with me." The old-world wonder you experienced when strolling among those rosebushes is attainable— it just takes some thoughtful planning to achieve.

QUESTIONS TO ASK
BEFORE YOU BEGIN

BEFORE YOU HEAD TO YOUR LOCAL GARDEN CENTER AND DESCEND on your backyard with bags of potting soil and an armful of rose plants, there are important considerations to make about your future rose garden.

WHERE DO YOU GET THE MOST SUNLIGHT?

Roses are sun lovers; there's really no such thing as giving a rosebush too much sun. At minimum, they will need to be planted in an area that gets six to eight hours of direct sunlight. Morning sun is ideal. So look around where you live and find a sunny, warm spot that's not obstructed by trees, vegetation, or your house.

I cannot stress this enough: Never plant roses in shade or partial shade. Roses grown in the shade or without a minimum of six hours of sun will grow and stretch to reach the sun, but they will not bloom often or thrive.

WHEN IN DOUBT, FACE SOUTH

Roses can perform well facing any direction if there aren't any buildings or trees obstructing their minimum six hours of full sunlight, but the most ideal orientation is south, and the least ideal is north. For example, if the front of your home faces south and you have a shallow backyard facing north, you should consider planting your roses in your front yard because they will have more abundant sunlight there. If you have a large area for planting with nothing around it, this won't apply to you.

WHAT PURPOSE DO YOU WANT YOUR ROSES TO SERVE?

Most rose varieties, with the exception of some climbers, will work well in a cutting garden. If you're planning to use roses as part of your overall landscaping scheme instead, here are some tips:

- Fragrant varieties with large blooms (such as David Austin English roses) are beautiful adjacent to seating areas where their scent can fill the air.

- Roses with prolific smaller blooms, like shrub roses, are ideal for covering a slope or sprawling as ground cover. They typically look best from a distance where the full visual impact can be seen, and so you don't notice the spent blooms as easily.

- Compact roses that bloom nonstop, such as floribundas, make beautiful additions to patios in containers. They provide immediate beauty when entering the garden.

- Thornless or nearly thornless roses such as Clouds of Glory (page 163) are wonderful along pathways.

- To create a barrier or hedge, plant multiple rose plants of the same variety very close together, about 18 inches (46 cm) apart. Floribunda and shrub roses would achieve this look the best.

- If you want to grow roses over a structure such as an arbor or trellis, choose a climbing variety.

WHAT VARIETIES OF ROSES DO YOU WANT TO GROW?

Whether you have a small patio and plan to plant your roses in containers or enjoy a large backyard with plenty of space for garden beds, it's important to make sure your rosebushes vary in shape and size. If you have five rosebushes or fifty, think of your garden bed in three tiers: The back of the bed should be home to your taller, more structured roses (like grandifloras and hybrid teas); the middle of the bed should feature lush, mid-height plants or roses (like English roses or shrub roses); in the front of your garden bed, you would plant smaller roses such as floribundas or miniatures. This planting approach creates a stacked, ascending look that's both aesthetically appealing and beneficial to the health and resilience of the plants. Following these principles also allows you to maximize your space for growing roses.

WHAT OTHER PLANTS DO YOU WANT TO GROW?

When you are choosing other plants to grow with your roses, there are several factors to consider: aesthetics (how the plants will look together), growing conditions (do they like the same soil moisture and sunlight?), and plant health (are they healthy and will they bring diseases to one another?).

Selecting companions that help keep pests at bay, improve soil, or have a beneficial effect on roses is a great way to grow roses organically. I tend to plant my roses with herbs like lavender, sage, and oregano. The herbs create a soft, whimsical look in the garden bed without competing with the rose plants in the way that flowering shrubs would. Herbs are also low maintenance while deterring pests. (Plants in the onion family, such as alliums and chives, will discourage aphids and disease as well.)

Companion planting can help with your garden design, too. As the growing season goes on, the foliage closest to the ground becomes less attractive than it was in the spring. Underplanting with companion plants can mask the unsightly foliage. (This is particularly the case for hybrid tea roses, which tend to have bare canes closest to the ground—also known as having "bare legs" in the gardening world.) Short, mounding, or spreading plants such as lavender and catmint will make nice partners for these roses. They will provide interest near the ground level to hide any bare canes and help suppress weeds. Annuals such as lantana and petunias are sun lovers that have similar watering and feeding requirements as roses and will also fill in a garden beautifully.

MY FAVORITE COMPANION PLANTS

Boxwood: Boxwood adds a touch of formal sophistication to a rose garden, and is easy to care for.

Geranium: My absolute favorite companion for roses is the geranium. True geraniums (perennials in the *Geranium* genus) have an intoxicating fragrance, and their foliage is such a pretty complement to roses when placed in a vase together. White and light pink geraniums will flower beautifully when given the same nutrients as roses.

Lantana: These colorful plants perennials will keep your garden vibrant in between rose flushes.

Lavender: Lavender looks lovely when paired with white or light pink roses. This companion is also helpful for attracting pollinators (bees) to your roses.

Leafy herbs: Sage, oregano, parsley, thyme, and mint will deter aphids and other pests from entering the garden while providing a farmhouse garden look. I prefer catmint over regular mint, as it is not as potentially invasive.

Petunia: Petunias make a sweet complement to roses and come in many colors.

Yarrow: These clusters of tiny, whimsical flowers attract ladybugs, which eat aphids.

TEN PLANTING PALETTES

CHOOSING COLORS THAT COMPLEMENT ONE ANOTHER
ensures your rose garden will look harmonious and pleasing to
the eye. Rose gardens look best when there are two complementary
colors of blooms and one accent color. Below are ten of my go-to
palettes, as showcased in the flower arrangements beginning on
page 280.

1. ELEGANT BLUSHES AND CREAMS

Blush   Cream   White

2. SPRING SHERBETS

Golden   Apricot   Coral

3. SUMMER PASTELS

Pink   Lavender   Mauve

4. PRETTY IN PINK

Light pink   Cotton candy   Salmon

5. EARTHY NEUTRALS

Mustard   Taupe   Dusty blush

6. PORCELAIN PALETTE

Ivory   Pure white   Champagne

7. WARM TO COOL

Peach   Lilac   Beige

8. ROUGE OPULENCE

Plum   Cherry   Currant

9. COTTAGE GARDEN

Blush   Pink   Raspberry

10. GARDEN ROMANCE

Blush to copper   French taupe   Magenta
ombré

CHAPTER FIVE

PLANTING

a

ROSE GARDEN

Once you've determined the best roses for your climate and your goals in planning your garden, it's time to get down to the specifics of planting your roses. Let's walk through each step of planting, from picking the right spot to spacing. We'll also discuss the adjustments you'll need to make if you're planting in raised beds or containers rather than planting in the ground. At the end of this chapter you'll be ready to plant and on your way to enjoying your roses.

PLANTING DIRECTLY IN THE GROUND OR IN RAISED BEDS

NOW THAT YOU'VE IDENTIFIED YOUR CLIMATE AND DECIDED WHAT rose varieties you wish to plant, it's time to start digging! The good news is that as long as they are planted in an area with at least six hours of direct sunlight per day (see page 214 for more on this), your roses will thrive in most any space or soil condition with sufficient drainage (see page 227). If you have a yard in which you plan to plant your roses, any grass will need to be removed permanently for the roses to thrive. Otherwise, the grass will grow up into your new rose beds; not only will it be unsightly but it will attract unwanted pests and disease. You can place weed barrier (landscape fabric) on top of your soil to keep grass and weeds at bay—cover it with mulch, so it's not seen.

A great alternative to planting roses in the ground is using raised beds, which can be made any shape to fit a garden. They are easy to move if necessary, and planting roses in them is much less back-breaking work than digging holes in the ground. Plus, caring for roses in a raised bed requires less stooping over.

To construct a wooden raised bed, use either redwood or cedar planks—neither of these types of lumber need to be treated with chemicals that may harm the roses. You can also use prefabricated corrugated metal planters. Whatever you choose for your raised bed, make sure it's at least 6 inches (15 cm) deep. Line the bottom of the raised bed with 0.5-inch (1 cm) chicken wire to keep gophers, moles, and voles out of your roses (a huge advantage over planting in the ground and constructing individual wire baskets for each rose). Fill with a balanced organic soil that contains compost.

PROTECTING YOUR ROSES FROM GOPHERS

While many pests take days or weeks to damage a rosebush, a gopher can eat the roots of a plant overnight. Planting a rosebush inside a wire basket that is nestled into the hole you dig for the plant can help ward off gophers and deter them from eating the roots.

LAYOUT AND SPACING OF YOUR ROSE PLANTS

WHEN YOU'RE PLANNING YOUR ROSE GARDEN, BE MINDFUL OF creating good airflow between the plants. Providing ample space for each rosebush will prevent disease and pests while achieving a cohesive and balanced visual display at the same time. In general, I like to plant one rose for every 10 to 12 square feet (3 to 4 sq m) of space. If you're planting a cutting garden, plant your bushes 4 feet (1.2 m) apart so you can walk around them to cut from them. If you want to create a hedge, plant your rosebushes closer together (but no tighter than 18 inches/46 cm apart).

For visual impact, small groupings of the same rose will make a big impression. I love to plant shrub and floribunda roses in threes (planting rosebushes in odd-numbered groups always looks more aesthetically appealing than planting in even-numbered groups). Most roses can be planted as close as 18 inches (46 cm) apart. When doing so, be sure to provide airflow through your roses by pruning out any crossing branches in the middle (more on pruning in chapter 6). Always consider what the maximum width of your plant could be by reading the labels of the varieties you choose and determine your spacing width based off those measurements.

SOIL AND AMENDMENTS

PEOPLE ARE ALWAYS WORRIED THAT THEIR SOIL WILL NOT BE good enough for roses. Let me be the first to tell you that roses will grow in any kind and quality of soil. I have tested this time and again over the years and I have never been proven wrong. But let's take a step back. Existing soil *can* be "good" or "bad." Soil that is considered good would be loamy and have great drainage (see page 227), and contain both beneficial microorganisms and organic matter. Bad soil would essentially be sandy, dry, or full of rocks and void of all life.

It's not so much how the soil starts that matters, though, but rather how it progresses. On our farm, because we fertilize our roses regularly, we are constantly feeding the soil. We have planted roses in the worst-looking soil you could imagine and those roses, when watered and fertilized properly, grew into mirror images of our roses planted in great soil. The key is providing your roses with the nutrients, water, and sunlight needed for them to thrive.

Here are some great amendments to use for soil preparation no matter the quality of your existing soil. When you feed your roses a mixture of the following organics, good soil will come along with time. Nothing in gardening happens overnight, so expect building good soil to be a process.

- **Alfalfa.** We give our roses alfalfa every spring. It is a great source of nitrogen as well as phosphorus, potassium, and triacontanol, which stimulates and regulates growth. You can purchase alfalfa as meal or pellets. After sprinkling alfalfa on the top of your soil, be sure to water very well so the nutrients can absorb properly into the soil.

- **Kelp meal.** Kelp, otherwise known as seaweed, is the primary ingredient in the fertilizer we use to feed our roses (more on this on page 250). Kelp meal is a slow-release potassium source that gives the soil vitamins, growth-promoting hormones, amino acids, and more than seventy chelated trace minerals.

- **Compost.** Compost is made from decomposed organic matter that increases microorganism activity and improves the quality of the soil. Think of compost as what makes your soil rich. It saves water, nourishes the soil, and helps the soil stay healthy. When choosing compost for roses, look for one with a base of cow manure and add it to your soil when planting.

Worm castings

Premixed organic soil amendment

Alfalfa

- **Worm castings.** Made of worm manure, worm castings are high in nutrients such as potassium, magnesium, calcium, and phosphorus and help roses thrive in several ways. They promote positive bacterial growth, help stimulate healthy root and plant growth, protect roses from diseases, and retain soil moisture while improving soil aeration. Throw a handful of worm castings in with your soil when planting.

- **Mycorrhizal fungi.** We plant all our roses with mycorrhizal fungi. It is expensive, but it will help your roses establish better root systems, meaning they will grow more vigorously, be more resistant to drought, and flower more abundantly. Strong roots encourage the uptake of nutrients from the soil.

- **Peat moss.** While peat moss isn't an amendment that provides nutrients, it absorbs minerals and trace elements from compost and other beneficial amendments, thereby helping to keep nutrients in the soil. Peat mining has been connected to the release of carbon dioxide, so if you're planning on having a sustainable garden, you should consider opting for a different soil amendment. Peat can be added to soil when planting or whenever you want to give your roses an extra boost.

- **Premixed organic soil amendment.** Your local garden center will carry bags of premixed fertilizer starters that include helpful ingredients such as potassium sulfate, feather meal, and many of the aforementioned amendments. Add this mix to your soil when planting to cross many beneficial soil additions off your list.

WHAT DOES "LOAMY" MEAN?

Soil that is loamy has equal parts sand and silt, and a smaller amount of clay. Because it has more sand than clay, water drains out of loamy soil more easily, ensuring the plants don't rot from staying moist for too long. The clay helps it retain nutrients, which in turn allows plants to benefit from them longer than if the soil were mostly sand or rock. Note: If you're not sure about the drainage of your soil, dig a hole, fill it with water, and come back in one hour. If all the water has drained out, you have a spot suitable for roses.

TESTING YOUR SOIL'S pH

If your plants are struggling, showing signs of distress such as brown spots on their leaves, you may want to test your soil pH. A healthy pH for roses should be around 6.5. You can collect a soil sample and send it off to be tested by a lab or use an at-home kit. Your local rose society, garden center, or nursery will be able to help you adjust the pH with some simple steps and answer any questions you may have about testing your soil's pH at home.

WATERING

THERE IS NO ONE "CORRECT" AMOUNT OF WATER TO GIVE A rosebush, because every environment is different. Even roses planted at homes next door to each other may have different water requirements! There are several factors that go into determining the amount of water your plant will need to thrive. Weather is the most variable consideration: Plants require more water during the hot summer months and less water when it's cooler or overcast during the day. Soil conditions will also play a big factor: If your soil isn't loamy (see page 227) and therefore doesn't drain well, you'll need to be careful not to overwater, as this can cause root rot. (You'll notice when the plant is getting too much water because the leaves will start to turn yellow, and the ground will be very wet.) Finally, roses in containers will require more frequent watering, as the sun tends to dry the soil much more quickly.

The easiest way to monitor your roses' water needs is to simply touch the soil. If it's dry, add water. If it's wet, skip a day—or more—as needed. You can also purchase an inexpensive soil probe that reads the moisture level. Until you're familiar with your rose plant and its individual needs, you must observe how it's reacting to the surrounding conditions. But don't worry, roses are very resilient plants and can produce beautiful blooms if adjustments are made.

WATER CONSERVATION

Our farm is in California, where we often deal with severe drought, and we take every measure possible to conserve water. The farm uses an automated system that connects to a weather station onsite and monitors the soil moisture. I can easily adjust the output of water and fertilizer as the climate and soil conditions change. For home gardeners, I highly recommend soil probes to monitor your plants' moisture needs. You can also add a thick layer of mulch around your bushes to help keep the soil cool and prevent water evaporation, as we do.

HOW TO WATER YOUR ROSES

If you live in an area with humidity but sporadic rainfall, you can rely on watering through a hose or watering can. But if you live in a dry area like a desert or Mediterranean climate, you'll want to install an irrigation or drip system. I highly recommend watering roses via a drip system and not sprinklers. Overhead watering can lead to mildew or blackspot and cause botrytis on the petals (more on these conditions on pages 245–247). If a drip system is not an option, make sure to only overhead water early enough in the day to allow for the leaves to dry out before the sun sets. My farm uses overhead watering as prevention against mites in the summer—in addition to a regular watering routine—but I do not rely on that water to nourish my plants.

PLANTING ROSES

THERE ARE TWO COMMON WAYS TO PURCHASE ROSES: AS BARE root roses—which are plants that have been pulled from the ground during winter or their dormancy and stripped of their leaves and blooms—or potted roses that you purchase in soil. Roses in soil can be immediately planted following the instructions on pages 232–235. To get bare root roses off to a fast start, plant them in a pot with light potting soil for three to six months before transplanting them into the ground. (The soil in the pot will be warmer than the ground because of the sun radiating around the pot. This stimulates fast root growth, which will result in the rose maturing more quickly than it would if planted in the ground.)

WHEN TO PLANT YOUR ROSES

Roses can technically be planted any time of the year, but the ideal time is early spring, and the least ideal is in the highest heat of the summer season. Most bare root roses are shipped by zone, so they're only available after the last frost of the season (or the early stages of spring) where you live. This can be anywhere from January to April, depending on your climate. If you're looking to plant roses that are already in soil, a garden center will typically have these available in early spring. You'll see that the selection of rose plants to purchase at your local garden centers and nurseries will narrow in the summer months.

GRAFTED OR OWN-ROOT

Most roses grown for home gardeners are created through a process called grafting. A rose is grafted when a grower fuses the plant tissue of one rose variety onto rootstock of a different variety. Own-root roses are grown from cuttings taken from a variety that is rooted in soil. These cuttings are then planted directly in the ground. Both types will give the gardener beautiful plants, and most gardeners do not have a preference (though if you're in a colder climate, such as Zone 3 or 4, you'll have better luck with own-root roses—see more on page 208). Typically, grafted roses are sold as two-year-old plants while own-root roses are sold at one year old, making them slightly smaller.

PLANTING ROSES IN THE GROUND OR A RAISED BED

STEP 1: Dig the hole for your rose plant. It should be at least 2 by 2 feet (0.6 by 0.6 m), or larger if your soil is very compact. If you're not sure about the drainage of the new location, dig your hole, fill it with water, and come back in one hour. If all the water has drained out, you have a spot suitable for roses.

STEP 2: Place your rose into the hole. In warm climates, make sure the crown (see page 15) is just above the top of the soil. In climates with freezing winters, bury the crown of the rose for winter protection. *If you're planting a potted rose plant*, squeeze the pot to loosen the plant, then place one hand over the surface and turn upside down so you can catch the plant as it slides from the pot. You want to keep the fine, hairlike roots intact, so be gentle when removing young roses from their pots. *If you're planting bare root roses*, set the plant in place so that the crown is at ground level. Backfill with half the soil that you dug up from the ground.

STEP 3: Add in equal parts mulch, potting soil, and a premixed organic starter fertilizer. When your hole is half full, water it to help the soil mixture settle. Then fill with the rest of your soil mixture and pat down. Water the rosebush well, and if the soil sinks a bit, add a little more soil or mulch on top. *If you're planting bare root roses*, mounding up mulch around the canes will help protect the newly planted rose from drying out. In dry climates, this is especially important. The rose cannot take up water into the canes until the roots have established. After about two weeks you can uncover the canes and they will start to put on new growth.

STEP 4: Continue to water your new rose plant every day for two weeks. Then begin a regular watering schedule (for more on watering, see page 228).

PLANTING ROSES IN CONTAINERS

You don't need to have a yard to grow roses. You can transform a deck, terrace, patio, or balcony into a sanctuary for roses—all you need is a sunny location (at least six hours of direct light) and enough room for a large container (at least 15 gallons/57 L). Roses in pots can live happily for years if their needs are met.

1. **Choose the right roses.** Compact, disease-resistant varieties with continual or repeating bloom perform best in pots. Avoid climbers, large shrub roses, grandifloras, and hybrid teas that are expected to grow very tall and wide. Floribundas are excellent choices, as are David Austin shrub roses, which stay around 3 feet (0.9 m) tall and wide. In the profiles beginning on page 27, I've indicated which varieties are best suited to container planting.

2. **Pick the right pot.** Grow roses in a container that holds at least 15 gallons (57 L). Wine barrels cut in half make wonderful pots for roses and hold 25 to 30 gallons (95 to 114 L). The larger your pot, the more your roses can grow. Make sure your chosen container has a drainage hole in the bottom.

3. **Create a healthy potting mix.** Use half compost and half potting mix or potting soil that's enriched with peat moss (see page 227). You can also mix in redwood mulch to regulate soil temperatures and conserve moisture. If you want to create your own potting mix from scratch, combine peat, perlite, sand, and fiber bark to make a lightweight, loamy soil for containers.

4. **Water regularly.** Potted roses will need more regular watering than roses planted in the ground. There are soil probes you can purchase to help you keep an eye on your soil's conditions. For a less formal measuring method, periodically stick your finger into the soil: If it is as wet as a wrung-out sponge, your rose is well watered. You don't want to let your potted roses dry out.

5. **Fertilize.** Feed your potted roses for the first time in spring, once they show new growth of about half an inch (1 cm), and then after each flush of blooms. For more blooms, you can fertilize every two weeks. Sprinkle an organic fertilizer on the soil and water in well. Always follow the recommendations on the fertilizer packaging.

PLANTING A CLIMBING ROSE

Climbing roses add a romantic, storybook charm to the garden, and once you've seen a rose climb and spill majestically over a structure, it's hard not to fall in love with this type of rose. Climbing roses grow vertically, typically up and over an architectural feature like an arch, arbor, or lattice. While climbing roses are very vigorous, they will take a couple of seasons to completely cover a structure. Don't give up on them—the reward of these dreamy roses is well worth the wait.

When planting a climbing rose, plant your bushes as close to the structure on which you want them to grow as possible. For example, if you're trying to cover an arch, you will put a rosebush on the outside edge of either side of the arch, centering the bush on each side. Train the canes up either side by affixing them to the structure with wire, ties, gardening tape, or zip ties.

As the plant continues to grow and spread its canes, you want to train them continuously in the direction you desire. This can involve training it in different places as the plant grows to achieve the shape you want, whether it goes up and over an arch, over the support of a gazebo, across a pasture fence, and so on. As the plant gets heavier and the canes mature, you may need to upgrade to sturdier attaching methods—for example, from green gardening tape to strong wire.

PEGGING CLIMBING ROSES

To maximize growth on climbing or rambling roses, you can try a technique called pegging. These roses tend to throw out very long shoots (called basal canes) from the crown of the rose at the base. When the canes or shoots feel pliable enough, you can bend the cane in a direction it would not naturally grow and carefully tie it to another cane. The tension of this technique will force the plant to throw new shoots and new growth on the upper side of the cane that is bent. This will make the plant look much fuller, and can result in a plant having ten times as many blooms than it would have before.

CHAPTER SIX

YEAR-ROUND ROSE CARE

There's a misconception that roses are finicky or difficult to grow and care for, but as someone who became an accidental rose farmer, I can attest to the ease of gardening roses once you've learned the ropes. The key is following a consistent care plan and routine and being proactive. Caring for roses is about thinking of what comes next—so if you're mindful of each season and what it brings, you will be successful.

ORGANIC PEST CONTROL
AND DISEASE MANAGEMENT

MANY YEARS AGO, WHEN MY HUSBAND AND I TOOK OUR HOME
rose garden to the next level and planted five hundred rose plants in our
backyard, I ended up taking a real-life crash course in pest management.
We got a horrible flower thrip infestation and had to completely disbud our
entire garden. I learned very quickly that a monoculture (where a significant
amount of one kind of crop is grown in one area) attracts far more pests
and disease than a garden that features a variety of plant species. The good
news for most home gardeners is that since you likely aren't planting a large
monoculture, you're probably not going to suffer from as many pests and
disease threats as we do at our farm. However, I've learned many tricks over
the years for preventing and combating both.

Much like humans, plants perform better when they're healthy. Plants
that are thriving, well fertilized, and properly watered will have a far better
chance of naturally fending off threats than sickly, struggling plants will. If
you plant varieties that are rated for growing in your zone (see page 206) and
give your roses what they need, they will put up a pretty good fight when
warding off diseases and pests.

USING YELLOW STICKY TRAPS

Yellow sticky traps attract aphids, whiteflies, mosquitoes, gnats, thrips,
leaf miners, fruit flies, leafhoppers, froghoppers, and other flying
insects. The traps are double-sided, and we staple them to 3-foot
(0.9 m) stakes that we push into the ground near any plants that seem
to be suffering from an infestation. The sticky surface of the yellow
traps not only eliminates adult insects caught there but also prevents
them from reproducing and creating more pests to deal with.

INTEGRATED PEST MANAGEMENT

My farm practices integrated pest management, an environmentally conscious approach to pest management that considers the life cycles of pests and how they interact with their environment. These are the factors you should consider for your own integrated pest management, which can easily be achieved on a smaller scale in a home garden:

1. **Choose rose varieties that are bred for your climate and have disease resistance.** Turn to page 206 to figure out what climate zone you live in. All of the rose varieties recommended in chapter 2 have strong disease resistance, and those that are especially hardy are noted as such.

2. **Grow your plants in healthy, balanced soil.** Turn to page 225 to review my favorite soil amendments.

3. **Trap pests to identify and control those that are impacting your roses.** Finding out which pests are eating your roses is crucial to understanding what treatment is needed. We use yellow sticky traps for this purpose (see opposite). Once the pests are stuck on the trap, we can see what is in our roses and how many of them there are, and come up with a plan to eradicate them (more on this on pages 241–244).

4. **Use beneficial insects to combat the pests you don't want on your roses.** It is helpful for growers to conserve the many natural pest enemies already at work in their fields and gardens. We use insects such as ladybugs and lacewings to eat aphids and keep the general pest population down. This is also called biological pest control—the act of employing living organisms to keep pests at bay.

5. **Implement an organic spray rotation.** There are three pesticides we incorporate in our disease and pest management: fungicides (to treat diseases like powdery mildew, rust, and blackspot), insecticides (to treat thrips and other insects), and miticides (to treat mites). You may prefer to use a product that treats for all three in one application—see more on page 248.

PESTS

NAME	WHAT THEY LOOK LIKE	WHAT THEY DO TO THE PLANT	TIME OF YEAR YOU SEE THEM	HOW TO PREVENT OR TREAT THEM
APHIDS	Tiny green or pink insects with soft, round bodies. Leave a trail of slimy, sticky substance.	Suck sap out of new growth, petals, and buds. Can cause leaves to curl.	Early spring and early fall	• Release beneficial insects like ladybugs or lacewings. • Spray them off with a garden hose. • Use neem oil or horticultural oil. • Spot-treat with pyrethrins if necessary.
CANE BORERS	Black insects about 0.25 inch (6 mm) long.	Bore holes in top of cane and leave larvae inside. Can cause yellow leaves and cane dieback.	Spring through fall	• Prune out the dead cane until you reach a section where the middle (pith) is white. Remove entire cane if necessary. Put multipurpose glue on top of cane after pruning.
EARWIGS (AKA PINCHER BUGS)	Insects with long, flat brown bodies, legs on the sides, and pinchers at the rear.	Create holes or ragged edges on the leaves or petals at night.	Late spring or early summer	• Prevent by keeping base of rosebush clean from debris, grass, and mulch when it's wet. • Use a spray with spinosad as the main ingredient. • Create an earwig trap by rolling up wet newspaper and letting it sit at base of plant overnight and then throwing it out in morning. The moist area will attract earwigs.

(continued)

NAME	WHAT THEY LOOK LIKE	WHAT THEY DO TO THE PLANT	TIME OF YEAR YOU SEE THEM	HOW TO PREVENT OR TREAT THEM
JAPANESE BEETLES	Insects with metallic blue-green bodies and tan wings, about 0.5 inch (13 mm) in size. The eggs are white and oval.	Leaves become skeletonized and fall off. Petals and buds are eaten by the beetles.	Early summer	• Pick them off with your fingers and dunk them in a bucket of soapy water. • Use neem oil. • Place Japanese beetle traps. • Use beneficial nematodes. • Use milky spore powder or granules to target beetles. • Spray with pyrethrins.
LEAFHOPPERS	Insects that are usually light green but can be brown or yellow. About 0.25 inch (6 mm) long.	Leaf discoloring. Can cause leaf to turn brown and fall off.	Late spring	• Release beneficial insects such as ladybugs and lacewings. • Keep garden clear of debris and excessive weeds. • Leafhoppers do not cause much damage to plants, so use organic sprays only as a last resort.
ROSE SCALE	Gray and white bumps on canes	Weakens plant growth and stunts blooms. Can cause cane dieback.	Early summer	• Use horticultural oil or insecticidal soap. • Release beneficial insects such as ladybugs, lacewings, and parasitic wasps. • Scrape off by hand. • Use sticky traps.

NAME	WHAT THEY LOOK LIKE	WHAT THEY DO TO THE PLANT	TIME OF YEAR YOU SEE THEM	HOW TO PREVENT OR TREAT THEM
SAWFLIES/ ROSESLUGS	Larvae resembling caterpillars. They are light green with yellow and black coloring, measuring about 1 inch (2.5 cm) long.	Eat holes in leaves and can skeletonize the leaves when infestations are large.	Spring	• Plant near flowers and plants that help control naturally, such as lavender, boxwood, marigolds, pansies, lantana, onions, and garlic. • Spray with products that have spinosad as an active ingredient. • Remove by hand. • Spray with water. • Release beneficial insects such as ladybugs or lacewings.
SPIDER MITES	Tiny black or brown spiderlike pests found on undersides of leaves and on canes.	Remove moisture from leaves and canes, causing leaves to turn yellow and fall off. In severe cases you'll see a webbing around affected areas.	During warm months, mainly in very dry areas	• Spray plants with a hose when weather is hot and dry. Focus on underside of leaves. • Release beneficial insects like lacewings. • Treat with insecticidal soap.
THRIPS	Minuscule black insects that scamper on the inside of developing buds.	Remove moisture from the petals and cause brown spots on them. In severe cases buds are deformed and blooms won't open.	Any time of year	• Be proactive, as thrips spread quickly! Apply organic pesticide, horticultural oil, or neem oil to help prevent thrips from invading rose blooms. • At the first sign of thrips, remove buds on affected plants and surrounding plants. • Place sticky thrip traps to attract insects away from blooms. • Release beneficial insects like lacewings.

PESTS

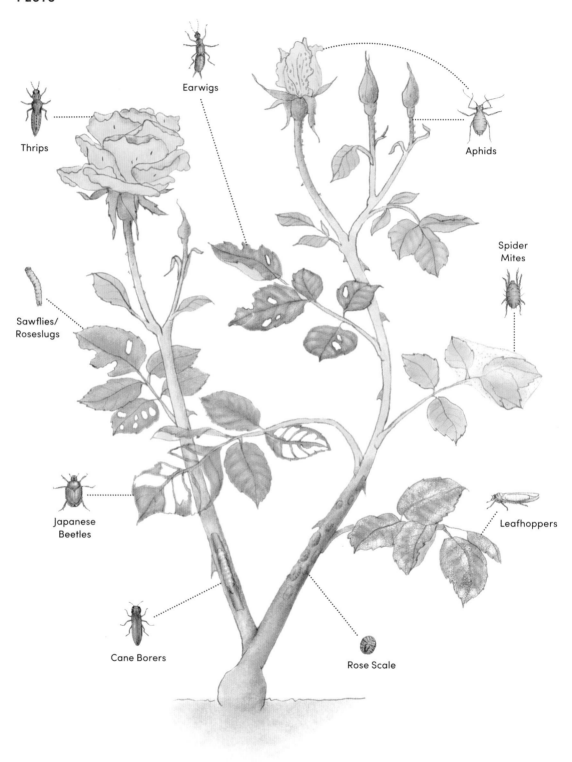

Earwigs

Thrips

Aphids

Spider
Mites

Sawflies/
Roseslugs

Japanese
Beetles

Leafhoppers

Cane Borers

Rose Scale

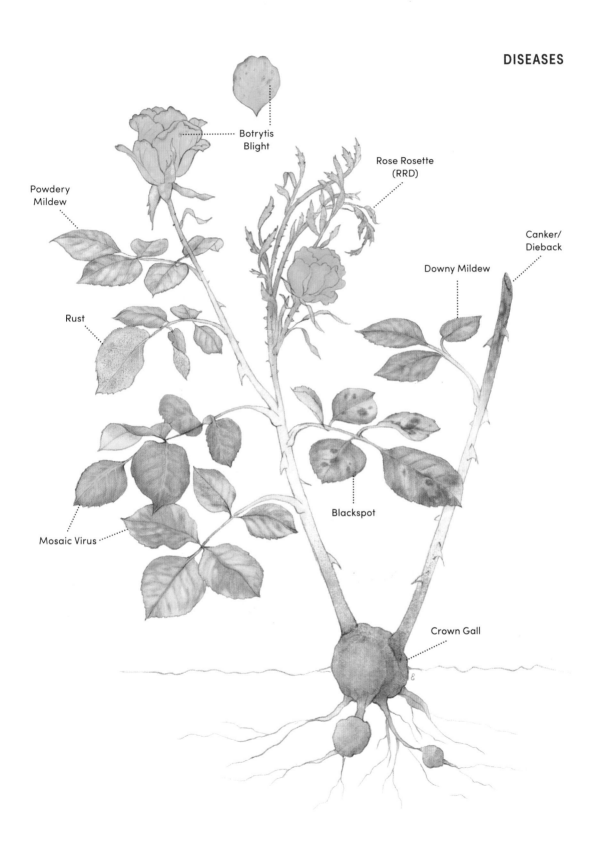

DISEASES

Botrytis
Blight

Rose Rosette
(RRD)

Powdery
Mildew

Canker/
Dieback

Downy Mildew

Rust

Blackspot

Mosaic Virus

Crown Gall

DISEASES

NAME	WHAT IT LOOKS LIKE	WHAT IT DOES TO THE PLANT	TIME OF YEAR YOU SEE IT	HOW TO PREVENT OR TREAT IT
BLACKSPOT	Circular black spots with feathery margins, often with yellowing around them	Causes leaves to turn yellow and fall off. Can cause cankers on the canes.	During wet weather	• Plant roses with sufficient space so foliage doesn't spread the disease. • Water roses using drip irrigation and avoid overhead watering.
BOTRYTIS BLIGHT	Pink spots on the petals, or tips of petals becoming soft and turning brown	Prevents blooms from opening and causes them to rot quickly. Can cause cane dieback.	Spring and fall	• Deadhead affected roses. • Provide air circulation by planting with sufficient spacing or pruning out infected canes. • Water roses using drip irrigation and avoid overhead watering.
CANKER/ DIEBACK	Starts as small dark or yellow spots on canes; as it progresses, canes can turn black. Lesions have a light gray or brown center surrounded by a dark purple or brown margin.	Causes dieback and can kill the rosebush.	Any time of year	• The most common cause of canker is dirty pruners, so disinfect them with bleach before use to reduce the chance of infection. If treating an infected plant, also disinfect pruners after use so as not to pass the infection along to another plant. • Avoid injury to plant and keep it healthy. • Remove infected portions of plant.
CROWN GALL	Brown, woody, tumorlike growth on base of plants	Weakens and stunts plant growth.	Any time of year	• Disinfect pruners with bleach before pruning as a preventive measure. • Remove infected plants.
DOWNY MILDEW	Yellow spots on leaves that turn to purple, red, or black	Causes defoliation, stunts growth, cracks canes.	Any time of year	• Plant roses with sufficient space so foliage doesn't spread the disease. • Water roses using drip irrigation and avoid overhead watering. • Remove affected leaves on plant and ground. • Prune diseased canes.

NAME	WHAT IT LOOKS LIKE	WHAT IT DOES TO THE PLANT	TIME OF YEAR YOU SEE IT	HOW TO PREVENT OR TREAT IT
MOSAIC VIRUS	Yellow patterns on leaves	Weakens plant growth and production. Can make plants more susceptible to other diseases.	Mostly occurs in spring but can occur at any time of year	• No known cure. • Doesn't transfer between plants, only when grafted onto healthy plants.
POWDERY MILDEW	White powder on leaves or canes, often on top of stems near base of blooms	Causes leaves and blooms to be deformed.	Most often spring and fall, but can appear any time of year when days are dry with humid and cool nights.	• Plant roses with sufficient space so foliage doesn't spread the disease. • Water roses using drip irrigation and avoid overhead watering. • Remove affected leaves. • Spray neem oil.
ROSE ROSETTE (RRD)	Deformed stems, leaves, and blooms; excessive thorns; thickened, fleshy canes; brushlike clusters; or red splotches on leaves. Also known as witch's broom.	Deforms plant and blooms.	Noticeable in spring but can appear at any time of year	• Remove affected rose and foliage as soon as possible. Start a preventive miticide regimen using bifenthrin or Forbid 4F, and spray general area, including nearby plants, after first flush, concluding at first frost. Roses may be replanted after 7 days if all traces of infected roses are removed. • Monitor nearby roses for signs of RRD.
RUST	Orange powder on underside of leaves, yellow spots on top side of leaves	Defoliates canes.	Spring and fall. Can occur in summer if conditions include mild temperatures with high moisture.	• Plant roses with sufficient space so foliage doesn't spread the disease. • Spray with organic fungicide as a preventive measure (this will not help the plant once symptoms appear). • Carefully remove affected leaves and put them in a trash bag to prevent from spreading. • Remove severely affected plants.

ALL-IN-ONE PESTICIDES

It can be prudent for home gardeners or growers to use a regular and preventive pesticide care routine to give their roses the best chance at vitality. Typically, an all-in-one pesticide takes the form of horticultural or neem oil. My farm uses the brands Suffoil-X and Tritek. For your home garden, look for Monterey Horticultural Oil and 70 percent neem oil. Be mindful that you cannot use one of these products exclusively because insects will become immune to them—alternate between the two for best results. Also note that in the summer months, oil-based pesticides can burn plants. To avoid this, I suggest spraying in the morning or stopping all spraying once temperatures reach 70°F (21°C).

FUNGICIDES

A fungicide will help you combat powdery mildew and rust. We see a lot of powdery mildew in the spring and fall, and plants are most susceptible to it on cool mornings or evenings when the plants remain moist and never completely dry out. Not only is powdery mildew unsightly, but in large quantities it can deform the top growth and buds. Rust will look like orange spots under the leaves of your roses. These are the products we use in rotation to ward off powdery mildew and rust:

- SaferGro Mildew Cure

- Cease

- Defender PM

- Kocide 3000

- Regalia

PESTICIDES AND MITICIDES

Whether you're battling flower thrips, aphids, spider mites, or other pests, the best thing you can do is start over with a clean slate. The most effective way to ensure that pests are removed from your garden is to cut off all the buds and blooms of your roses and start fresh. Make sure you bag up the cut blooms and buds and put them in the trash. Once you've eradicated your pests, you can give your plants a new chance to thrive with prevention in place. These are the pesticides and miticides we like to use:

- Captain Jack's Deadbug Brew

- BotaniGard ES

- Debug Turbo

- PyGanic

- Brandt Ecotec Plus

- Entrust SC Naturalyte

SPEAK WITH LOCAL GROWERS

At the end of the day, the best resource for finding the right prevention approach for your home garden is your local rosarians, rose society, or garden center. Wherever you live, the people who are experts at growing roses in your area will know the pests and diseases you might encounter and the best ways to keep them out of your garden.

HOW TO HAVE A NO-SPRAY GARDEN

While spraying is essential for my own rose-growing business and many home gardeners prefer to spray, some gardeners opt to have a "no-spray" garden—they don't want to apply any pesticides, fungicides, or miticides to ward off pests and diseases. If you choose not to spray in your garden, you need to be prepared to put in more preventive effort with your rose plants.

First and foremost, if you live in an area that has a very moist climate, it is crucial that you choose varieties that are disease resistant. Plants that are labeled as disease resistant will not be threatened by fungal diseases such as blackspot, mildew, or rust. Second, feeding your roses organic material like alfalfa will make them heartier, enabling them to ward off pests and diseases. Think of your soil as being like the immune system of the human body— the healthier the immune system, the more effectively it can fight illness. Using organic mulch and compost to feed and enrich your soil will also fortify your rose plants against pests and diseases. Additionally, grow companion plants in your garden that will attract beneficial insects that will eat aphids, thrips, and other pests. Echinacea and other herbs and flowers make great companion plants for this purpose.

Lastly, if your preference is to keep your pest and disease approach simpler, you can use horticultural oil and copper. Both are effective and natural. Stay vigilant with your roses and check them regularly for any signs of pests or diseases.

FERTILIZING

A CONSISTENT FERTILIZING ROUTINE IS KEY IN HELPING A ROSE plant bloom, maintain lush foliage, and keep away pests. The more nutrient-rich your soil is, the better your roses will perform and thrive.

There isn't one tried-and-true way to properly fertilize a rose plant—in fact, there are several different effective methods (see page 226 for soil amendment suggestions). So if you're growing roses for the first time, I recommend you experiment with a few different approaches, observe how your plants react to them, and stick with the one that makes them the happiest. Record your experiments and their results so you can measure the success of your efforts. Trust me, you'll know when your rose plants really take to a particular fertilizing plan.

While some may tout the benefits of synthetic fertilizers, we've always chosen to use organic fertilizers with our rose plants—specifically, fertilizer tea. To make it, fill a clean 55-gallon (208 L) trash can most of the way with water and add roughly half a gallon (2 L) of alfalfa pellets (see page 226). Place the lid back on the trash can and let it sit in the sun for a few days. After this process you can mix in fish emulsion or other water-soluble organic fertilizers to provide additional nutrients to your plants. Then either fill buckets with the tea and pour a gallon (4 L) of the liquid on each plant or spray the tea from the trash can with a sump pump onto your plants. This by no means smells great, but the roses absolutely love it!

Another option is to use a "fertigation" injection system like EZ-FLO, which offers a low-maintenance approach to watering and fertilizing.

WHEN SHOULD I FERTILIZE MY ROSES?

We always do our first fertilization of the year in the spring, after the rose plant has a few inches (8 cm) of new growth. If you live in an area that gets frost, your first fertilization of the year will occur after the last frost of the winter. If you live in the United States, this is an easy fertilizer schedule to remember: Easter (April), Memorial Day (late May), Fourth of July, and Labor Day (September).

SIGNS OF PLANT DEFICIENCY

A rosebush is telling you it needs more attention if leaves start to change colors or shapes. A yellow leaf can mean either too much water or too little. Check the soil and drainage around the plant to determine if either is your problem. A yellow leaf can also mean a lack of nitrogen. Using a foliar fertilizer high in nitrogen (more on foliar fertilizer on page 263) or adding alfalfa or organic compost to the soil will help increase nitrogen in the plant. Yellowing or chlorotic leaves can also indicate an iron deficiency. If you see a deficiency in your rosebush's leaves, consult with your local rose society to determine what your plant is telling you and how to remedy the problem.

A rosebush with an iron deficiency will show a lack of chlorophyll in the leaves. Adding chelated iron to the soil will help chlorotic leaves retain their green color.

SPRING PRUNING

THE FORSYTHIA BLOOMING (USUALLY IN LATE MARCH), FOR MANY gardeners and growers, is nature's sign that winter is on its way out and spring is on its way in. It's a collective sigh of relief that there likely won't be another heavy frost. This is also a sign to rose gardeners that it's safe to prune their roses and begin their season.

A rosebush stays dormant until it is pruned. Cutting the canes off the plant sends a message to the rosebush to wake up and start growing. So, no matter where you live, if your area has seen its last frost of the season, the minute you prune your roses is when your rose growing season begins. If you live in a warmer area, you might prune your roses as early as January or February (in Zone 10, where I live, rose pruning is done by the end of January so my roses will flush in early April). People in places that see moderately cold weather will prune their roses two to four weeks before their last frost. And if you live someplace that sees very cold temperatures, you'll prune your roses after your last frost date (if roses are pruned too early in cold areas, new growth could be susceptible to frost damage). In the US, following the *Old Farmer's Almanac* frost dates should give you a good prediction for when you'll want to prune your roses for the growing season.

Another sign it's time to prune is when you see buds swelling on your rose canes (as shown at right). This means the roses are waking from their winter dormancy and are starting to push new growth.

Swelling buds on a
rosebush's canes in spring

WHEN TO PRUNE IN YOUR ZONE

ZONE 10	January
ZONE 9	February
ZONE 8	Late February or March
ZONE 7	March
ZONES 5 AND 6	April
ZONES 3 AND 4	May

PRUNING A CLIMBING ROSE

It is important to note that climbing roses do not need to be pruned back heavily in the winter like other rose types do. If you did, you would lose all the structure you gained from the past year of growth. Instead, when you prune your climbing roses you will gently prune the canes in the spring while leaving the structure of the plant alone.

If you don't care for a wilder look, you can cut back the canes in the middle of the season. In midsummer, cut back your roses to reshape the plant. It will keep the plant from being so free flowing while reinforcing the shape.

HOW TO PRUNE YOUR ROSES

Pruning can feel very overwhelming to new rose gardeners, but I promise you this: You cannot mess this up and you won't kill your plants! Simply speaking, pruning is removing old, spent, spindly, or diseased wood from your roses. If it looks bad, cut it off; if it looks healthy, keep it. At our farm, we typically keep six to nine healthy canes for each of our rosebushes, and we only trim growth that doesn't appear to be healthy. When pruning, make sure to use bypass pruners and loppers that are clean and sharp.

WHAT YOU'LL NEED:

- Pruning gloves (ideally made of leather or vegan leather gauntlet)

- Loppers

- Felco or similar bypass pruners

STEP 1: Remove the top of the plant using loppers, leaving 18 to 24 inches (46 to 61 cm) of canes. This will make it easier to fine-tune the shape of the plants. By this time of year, many roses will be 5 to 8 feet (1.5 to 2.4 m) tall. Cutting back the top of the plant helps you see into the bush better to determine where to prune.

NOTE: If your roses are only a year or two old, you don't need to prune as much as you would with more established rose plants. Gently cut back the top of the plant by removing the thinnest growth. Leave as many healthy canes as possible and remove all foliage.

STEP 2: Using loppers, remove any wood that looks unhealthy, canes that are touching or crossing through the middle of the plant, and canes that are narrower than a pencil. Cut canes back to the crown (see page 15) and remove two or three canes. You can distinguish healthy canes from dying canes by looking for bud eyes (see page 15)—healthy canes will have bud eyes on them. This step helps shape your rosebush, and when done, it should look like a basket with all canes radiating outward from the base of the plant. Removing crossing branches creates better air circulation inside the plant.

STEP 4: Look for outward-facing bud eyes and make a 45-degree angle cut half an inch (1 cm) above the bud eye of each cane. This is where the new growth will occur next spring, and this cut will encourage the plant to grow outward, not inward.

STEP 5: The finished product should look almost like an open baseball glove, with the pruned canes fanning out from a central point. Discard all cuttings and removed leaves. Do not use rose debris as mulch or compost—it can carry diseases and pests.

STEP 3: Remove all leaves from the canes.

DISBUDDING

IF YOU'VE PLANTED A NEW ROSE PLANT—WHETHER IT'S BARE root or grafted—it could take some time before you have stems that are ready to harvest. If you allow buds to form and bloom on an immature rose plant, the stems won't be long or strong enough to cut. The solution is to disbud the plant, removing buds that are forming, which tells the plant to focus on growing instead of flowering.

At my farm, we routinely disbud our newer roses for one or two bloom cycles in the spring (for me this is in April and May) to establish hearty canes and strong roots. If you live in a cooler climate, you may want to disbud your rose plant for an entire growing season (not letting any blooms form) to help the plant take on the sturdy and hearty structure needed for prolific blooms the following season.

SUMMER DEADHEADING

DEADHEADING YOUR ROSES ONCE THE BLOOMS ARE SPENT WILL manipulate the plant to produce more flowers, resulting in more roses for cutting and enjoying (plus it looks tidier!). To deadhead a rose, grab a bucket, a pair of gardening gloves, and some sharp, clean gardening shears. Cut the stem of the spent bloom above the five-leaflet leaf set, making sure you leave buds that are still forming and yet to flower.

WINTER DORMANCY CARE

I LIKE TO THINK OF WINTER AS THE WORK SEASON, WHEN WE take each necessary step toward ensuring the following growing season will bring forth splendid, prolific blooms. In colder climates, your roses spend the winter under snow while you make your plans for the spring season. This is a great time to research and plan any new roses or companion plants you'd like to add to your garden in the spring. Once the last frost has come and gone, it's time to get outside and take stock of your garden. Cleaning up your beds, making sure your irrigation works, transplanting (if necessary), and pruning are all crucial to ensuring your garden is successful.

TRANSPLANTING

SINCE WE STARTED GRACE ROSE FARM MORE THAN EIGHT YEARS ago, we have transplanted thousands of roses—some of them more than once! Sometimes roses will outgrow their location and need to be moved to a different area in the garden where they can spread out. And of course, if you need to relocate your garden bed or move out of your home, your roses will need to be transplanted. While roses are adaptable, moving them should be done with care.

The best time to transplant a rosebush is when it's not actively growing. Moving a plant while it is dormant will mitigate the chance of shock. This means that if you are in an area that doesn't freeze, the best time to transplant your roses is in the late fall or winter. If you live in an area that experiences frost, transplant in early spring.

TRANSPLANTING DURING THE GROWING SEASON

There are times when we need to move a rosebush during the growing season, and while it's not ideal, it can be done. The biggest consideration is trying to keep your roses from going into shock. When roses' roots are exposed and cut, there is almost no amount of water that they can drink to prevent wilting at the top of the plant. You will want to water heavily for at least three days prior to moving your rose. A fully hydrated rose will lessen the demands on the roots because the roots will have to do less work extracting naturally occurring moisture from the soil.

In this case, it's preferable to cut the rose plant back by 50 percent, or no taller than 2 feet (0.6 m), before transplanting. If you elect not to prune down the rose, you'll need to watch carefully for wilted top growth. (Remove any top growth that wilts and becomes crispy.) After replanting, water heavily—at least once a day—until the rose is established. It will perk up, starting to push new growth, and its leaves will not be wilted. It will take up to six weeks for a rose to establish in a new spot within the garden.

HOW TO TRANSPLANT YOUR ROSES

STEP 1: Cut the rose canes back to about 12 inches (30 cm) from the crown and remove all foliage, if there is any. The plant should look bare.

STEP 2: When removing your rose from its current location, dig as far away from the root ball (where the muddy soil sticks to the roots) as possible. Preserving as much of the rose's root system as you can is key. Once the rosebush is removed from the ground, the plant becomes perishable and is at risk of drying out and dying. If you're moving far away from where the rosebush is currently planted or know it will not be replanted right away, dig up the plant, leaving as much soil around the root ball as possible. Spray down the root ball with water to keep the soil moist and wrap it in burlap for transport.

STEP 3: Dig a new hole for your rose and make sure that there is good drainage. If you're not sure about the drainage of the new location, dig your hole, fill it with water, and come back in an hour. If all the water has drained out, you have a spot suitable for roses. If your location is not suitable for planting, plant your rose in a container or raised bed with new potting soil and be sure to mix in organic compost.

STEP 4: Place your rose into the new hole and backfill with half the soil from the ground that you dug up. Water it in to help the soil mixture settle. Then add in equal parts of mulch, potting soil, and organic starter fertilizer. Add the rest of your soil mixture, pat it down, and water in well. Continue to water your newly transplanted rose every other day.

YEAR-ROUND ROSE CARE PLAN

GROWING BEAUTIFUL ROSES IS SOMETHING ANYONE CAN DO, NO
matter their skill level. On the pages that follow, I've outlined a rose care plan
to bring you success in the garden.

Note: I've based the monthly breakdown on my own zone (10), so you may
need to shift each month's directives forward or backward up to a few months
depending on the zone you live in. Consider "January" below as the end of
frost, or when you start to see new growth on your rose plants.

JANUARY

I think of January as a work month. While there isn't instant gratification for the effort you put in this month, your labor will pay off in a few short months when your roses are performing beautifully.

Bare Root Rose Planting: Any bare root roses should be planted as quickly as possible. Once they arrive from the grower, they need to be placed in a bucket of water to soak. You can add a scant tablespoon of vitamin B_1 (for root growth stimulation) and the same amount of bleach (to avoid root gall, downy mildew, and other diseases) per gallon (3.8 L) of water. Allow bare root roses to soak for twenty-four hours before planting.

Pruning and Dormant Spraying: Prune and clean up the debris from your roses. This is also a good time to make sure your drip irrigation emitters are working. The garden bed should be clean when you finish with pruning. For dormant spraying, we do this about a week after pruning. We use horticultural oil, copper, and a surfactant, which helps products stick to the plant for ideal penetration. Repeat two weeks later.

Apply Granular Rose Food to the Roses: After pruning and cleaning up all rose debris, give established rosebushes ¼ cup (59 ml) of dry granular fertilizer and water it in well. We also like to give our roses alfalfa in January as it will break down over time and begin feeding our roses once the soil warms up.

Finish Planting with Mulch: Mulching is an important last step in winter rose care. Mulch can be purchased from your city or county or from your local garden center in bags. Any double-steamed mulch is perfect for roses.

FEBRUARY

February is when our roses will start to show new growth. It's an exciting time in the garden. All that fresh, tender new foliage is perfect, and you want to keep it that way. About three to four weeks after pruning, bud eyes (see page 15) will emerge, which is just the start of what's to come.

The First Feeding: As soon as you see new growth on your roses, you can start to feed them. We do this with our irrigation system, but you can just as easily feed manually. An application of fish emulsion, a scoop of compost, alfalfa, and granular organic fertilizer is what we use in early spring. You cannot overfeed roses that are established when using organic fertilizers.

Monitor Roses for Disease and Pests: We begin to see aphids and powdery mildew toward the end of February. It is much easier to prevent powdery mildew than it is to eliminate it after roses have it. Using an organic fungicide to prevent diseases such as powdery mildew, blackspot, and rust can be done in February at half strength so as not to burn new foliage. You can also wash down your roses early in the day to control pests such as aphids.

MARCH

March holds the promise of spring, and blooms are right around the corner. This is a month of great anticipation for rose growers!

Continue Feeding: March is when we get into the routine of feeding our roses weekly, giving the plants small amounts of fertilizer on a regular basis while they're being watered.

Monitor for Pests and Diseases: If you use a fungicide to prevent powdery mildew, it will need to be sprayed every seven to ten days depending on how much mildew your garden gets. We have some roses that require routine disease prevention. Others will never get powdery mildew due to their disease resistance. Use as directed on the product label.

March is when aphids will make your roses their home. They love to suck the juice out of new foliage and blooms, and they leave a sticky residue on roses. They can be controlled with insecticide or just washed off the roses with the jet option on a hose end sprayer. Aphids will die when they fall off the rose and hit the ground.

Snails love roses as much as the next pest. Snail bait can be applied around roses to keep their populations down. We don't have many snails where we farm, so we don't have to do any preventive measures. Use snail bait with care around children and animals.

We will also begin to see earwigs this time of year. We have a commercial pest control company visit the farm to apply insecticides around our buildings and farm. Earwigs are terrible pests once they get into our roses, so we stay on top of them with the pest control company.

APRIL

April is the most beautiful month for roses. They burst so quickly that we can't keep up with them! There is no denying that the first flush of blooms in the spring is a sight to behold. There is a purity and freshness to April roses that we don't see in other months. April is also when the weather starts to warm up and our roses require more from us to stay beautiful.

Continue Fertilizing and Monitor for Spider Mites: As the days get warmer and drier, spider mites can make their way into roses. Spider mites can be prevented with daily washing of the foliage on the undersides with a hose, or by using a miticide. Spider mites can and will destroy a rosebush, so it's important to watch for them and treat quickly. We try to stay ahead of spider mites because we have lost entire bloom cycles to them in the past.

Keep an Eye out for Balling: This is important to monitor all year, but rose blooms can ball especially in the spring when the weather is moist and rain can weigh down the petals. A rose bloom will ball and not open up fully when it is humid and heavy with moisture. To prevent balling, make sure your rosebushes have plenty of space between them and prune the canes regularly. Remove any blooms that have already balled.

MAY TO AUGUST

Late spring and summer are great times for roses. Continuing to feed roses routinely throughout this growing period will result in big, healthy plants.

Deadhead and Anticipate the Next Bloom Cycle: By the middle of May, most of our roses are preparing for their second bloom cycle. We deadhead any spent blooms that didn't get harvested.

Maintain the Health of Your Garden: This is the time of year when we gradually increase our watering and watch our plants closely for western flower thrips. Routine spraying of organic pesticides will prevent any outbreaks. Once thrips are in our roses, it's nearly impossible to eradicate them. Along with our spray regimen, we will typically give the roses a foliar fertilizer, which helps them green up and look their best. This is the process of spraying the plant leaves directly with a fertilizer, so the nutrients are absorbed through the foliage. Common organic fertilizers are compost tea, kelp, fish, and bone meal.

Fortify Your Plants for Continuous Blooms: We feed our roses with seaweed and fish emulsion-based fertilizers every time we water.

Keep an Eye out for Caterpillars: In late summer we experience rose caterpillars, which are the grossest of all the pests. They will take over a garden of roses incredibly quickly, so it's very important to watch for any signs of these small green creatures in the buds of the roses.

SEPTEMBER AND OCTOBER

The biggest change we experience in the early fall is the presence of powdery mildew creeping its way back onto our roses. Once mildew is in our roses it's very hard to eradicate, so we spray preventively. We do not deal with many pests after the height of summer if we routinely check our plants for problems that may arise.

Stick to Your Watering Routine: Since it's very hot where we farm, we continue to water and feed our roses just as we do all summer. They love the warm days and bloom generously this time of year.

NOVEMBER AND DECEMBER

Because of where we farm, we are still harvesting roses through December. With the decreased daylight and cooler temperatures, our roses will gradually slow down. They never quit fully, but by mid-December they are tired and ready for a rest.

Start Scaling Back Your Watering and Fertilizing Schedule: By this time of year, we usually have a day or two of rain, so we don't need to water as frequently. We also back off on the fertilizing as a way of telling our roses that it's okay to start preparing for their winter nap.

Part Three

HARVESTING

and

ARRANGING

ROSES

CHAPTER SEVEN

HARVESTING ROSES

One of the many joys of having a rose garden is bringing cut roses inside to behold, their intoxicating scent a testament to all the work and care you put into your plants. The mood of a room is instantly brightened with fresh flowers, and there is nothing more satisfying than enjoying the fruits of your labor. At Grace Rose Farm we harvest blooms seven days a week for nine months out of the year. Through our experience gathering millions of roses a year, we've developed trusted methods for harvesting roses that give them lasting beauty in a vase once cut from the plant.

AT WHAT STAGE TO HARVEST

IF A ROSE IS CUT TOO EARLY, IT WON'T BE MATURE ENOUGH TO open on its own once it is placed in water. Conversely, if you harvest a rose when the bloom is already blown out, it will last for a day or two at most after being cut and placed in a vase. Knowing the right time to harvest roses is essential to ensuring you can enjoy your cut flowers in your home for as long as possible.

Too early   Time to harvest

WHEN TO HARVEST

ROSES ARE VERY SIMILAR TO HUMANS IN THAT THE MORE hydrated they are, the better they perform. Harvesting first thing in the morning, when there's the most moisture in the rose stem, is ideal. This is the time of the morning when the dew is glistening on the plants; the stem and tissue of the plant are in turn happily swollen from drinking up that moisture. As the day goes on, sunlight pulls moisture away from the rose—if you were to cut a rose in the afternoon on a sweltering summer day, you would probably have a limp bloom and stem.

TAKING STOCK OF YOUR ROSE PLANTS

An important part of harvesting is using the time you're near your plants to assess their overall health and see how they're growing. This is a great opportunity to make sure your rose plants don't have any pests or diseases, check that they're receiving enough water, and pick off any foliage or buds that are not in good shape.

WHAT YOU'LL NEED

- Clean, sharp bypass shears (such as a Felco 1 or 2)

- Protective gloves

- A clean bucket of fresh water

USE CLEAN TOOLS

If your pruners, shears, or any other gardening tools are gunky or dirty when you slice into a rose stem, you're going to introduce bacteria into the stem. This will cause the cut flower to have a shorter vase life.

STEP 1: First thing in the morning, look for roses with the sepals pointed down in the late bud stage.

STEP 2: Cut a 12-inch (30 cm) stem, leaving 2 to 3 inches (5 to 8 cm) of stem behind on the plant.

STEP 3: Remove any unsightly outer petals. Leave the top three leaflets on the rose: left, right, left of the upper leaves. Clean off all remaining foliage to ensure the water will remain clean.

STEP 4: Immediately place your cut stems into your bucket of fresh water—ideally no more than two minutes after cutting the stem from the plant. Allow your cut roses to take in water for at least one hour before trimming them to your preferred height and transferring to a vase or vessel (see page 272 for more).

Readying your freshly harvested roses for the vase should not be a rushed task. If you spend a few minutes taking the right precautions, you can ensure your cut stems last for as long as possible in your home.

STEP 1: Make sure your bypass pruners or shears are clean and sharp. Scissors are not sharp enough to slice the stem without crushing it, so ensure you have the right tools before you get started.

STEP 2: Cut the bottom of each stem at a 45-degree angle. This will ensure that it can drink water efficiently.

CHAPTER EIGHT

ARRANGING ROSES

Once your roses have started to set buds for spring, you can expect to see your first blooms within three weeks. This is a joyous time in the garden that reflects the work and dedication you put into your plants, and you can finally bring your roses into the home. Whether you harvest blooms for a simple arrangement or plan a rose-centered tablescape for a summer dinner party, there are many ways to transport the rose garden to your daily moments, celebrations, and everything in between.

THE FUNDAMENTALS OF ARRANGING ROSES

STEP 1: Choose a vessel that is wide enough for the number of stems you're working with. Fluff the roses in the vase and ensure their heads aren't smashed together—the looser they are in the vase, the more space the blooms have to open. If your stems feel cramped, opt for a larger vessel. Once you've chosen your vessel, clean and fill it with fresh water.

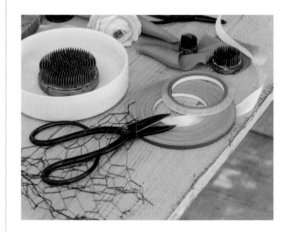

STEP 2: You may wish to add support to your vessel to keep your stems in place. If you're working with a clear vase, create a grid across the mouth of the vessel using clear floral tape. If you're using an opaque vessel, you could also use bunched-up chicken wire or a flower frog. Make sure to tape down your bunched-up wire with two pieces of floral tape across the top of the vessel in a cross shape. If using a frog, you'll need to keep the weight of your arrangement balanced or your frog will tip.

STEP 3: Now it's time to add stems to your vase. Make sure there aren't any leaves below the water line—they will deteriorate and shorten the life span of your arrangement. Start with greens (or filler), if using. These will create support in your vessel for the larger blooms. Then add your roses, starting with the shortest stems and building up to the tallest. This will help create an internal structure for your longer stems and support them as you build out the arrangement. Cluster two or three stems of the same rose variety together to mimic how roses grow on the plant. This helps create a natural-looking arrangement.

NOTE: You can create a bridge between different-colored varieties by incorporating roses that transition from one hue to another (for example, adding Connie's Sandstorm, which has petals that fall across the ombré spectrum from golden honey to rich mauve, to an arrangement of other yellow and purple varieties).

STEP 4: Continue adding layers of flowers in a "push and pull" system: As you add stems to your vessel, you will want the heights to vary from one bloom to the next. Pull stems out a bit or push them deeper into your vessel to create a dimensional look that mimics how flowers grow in nature. Another way to add dimension to the arrangement is to prevent the heads of the flowers from touching, instead letting each one exist on its own plane.

MONOCHROMATIC ARRANGEMENTS

WHILE MIXING DIFFERENT COLORS AND VARIETIES IS BEAUTIFUL and a fun exercise in creativity, you can't go wrong with a monochromatic arrangement. Come harvest time, cut multiple stems from the same variety to make a simple yet stunning arrangement in one hue. Place them together in a vessel, or arrange them in a grouping of smaller vessels for added drama.

TEN TIMELESS COLOR PALETTES

DRAWING FROM THE PLANTING PALETTES IN CHAPTER 4, creating a cohesive and appealing bouquet or arrangement should come easily. Here are ten of my favorite color combinations.

FEATURING:

Francis Meilland (page 69)

Tranquillity (page 167)

Clouds of Glory (page 163)

Iceberg (page 157)

Jasmine vine

Astilbe

If I had to gather up a bouquet of classic roses that still make me swoon after seeing them countless times over, this would be it. Francis Meilland and Clouds of Glory are known showstoppers with large, breathtaking blooms, and serve as the elegant anchors of the arrangement. Tranquillity and Iceberg provide tonal shifts and different petal counts in their smaller blooms, adding variety. A sprinkling of jasmine vine and astilbe give the whole arrangement movement and the perfect touch of green.

FEATURING:

Soul Sister (page 30)
Golden Celebration (page 192)
Marc Chagall (page 99)
Carding Mill (page 38)
Seasonal foliage

A floral arrangement that looks sweet enough to eat! Lean into the cheerful, bright hues of rose varieties like Soul Sister, Golden Celebration, Marc Chagall, and Carding Mill to build a vase full of sunshine. These vibrant, sherbet-colored roses are similar in bloom size, so they create a bountiful, satisfying sight in the vase all together. Add a sprig or two of seasonal foliage to give the grouping some additional movement.

FEATURING:

Love Song (page 121)

Stainless Steel (page 129)

Plum Perfect (page 118)

Boscobel (page 80)

Blush or white astilbe

Larkspur

Lavender sweet peas

Scabiosa

Seasonal foliage

When I think of summer, I think of an array of pastel colors mingling in the garden. For an arrangement with a more modern look, combine purple- and pink-toned roses in a low, bowl-shaped vessel. Wild-looking accent flowers will help the arrangement dance cheerfully, as will any pretty seasonal foliage that you can snip from the garden.

FEATURING:

Alnwick Rose (page 104)
Carding Mill (page 38)
The Lady Gardener (page 94)
Blush sweet peas

Everyone at my farm knows that I'm a pink rose girl, through and through. This arrangement is a celebration of some of my favorite varieties. These roses range from ballet-slipper pink to cotton candy pink to salmon, resulting in a joyful grouping of warm pink tones. A few blush sweet peas will add a flutter of movement.

FEATURING:

Honey Dijon (page 191)

Koko Loko (page 130)

Connie's Sandstorm (page 133)

Sweet peas

The rose varieties in this palette look may not scream *color*, but their subtle hues echo each other's tones, creating an elegant, subdued arrangement. A wisp or two of sweet peas complete this earthy grouping by adding texture and height.

FEATURING:

Lichfield Angel (page 164)
Pure Perfume (page 178)
French Lace (page 172)
Astilbe
White geranium
Seasonal foliage

There's something very classic and picturesque about a bouquet of white roses. To create an arrangement that's full of depth and interest, gather Lichfield Angel, Pure Perfume, and French Lace roses. These varieties may each appear to be "white" upon first glance, but they offer subtle tonal shifts from cream to apricot-tinged white. Including astilbe, white geranium, and seasonal foliage will complement the roses while adding a sense of movement and a sculptural quality to the arrangement.

FEATURING:

Koko Loko (page 130)

Love Song (page 121)

Princess Charlene de Monaco
(page 61)

Peach stock

This arrangement combines Koko Loko, Love Song, and Princess Charlene de Monaco. Koko Loko serves as the visual bridge between the warm pink of Princess Charlene and the cool purple of Love Song, resulting in a bouquet that's as interesting as it is sweet. Add in some peach stock to take the display to the next level—and place your stems in a pitcher for a special departure from your typical vase.

FEATURING:

Ingrid Bergman (page 146)

Darcey Bussell (page 122)

Traviata (page 141)

Munstead Wood (page 144)

Put a unique twist on a traditional red arrangement by gathering varieties in slightly different shades and using a collection of smaller vintage vessels rather than a single large vase. Seek out different shapes and sizes in the same material to maintain cohesion across the groupings in your display.

These are varieties that have charmed rosarians for years, bringing an old-fashioned splendor to the garden in their varying tones. A smattering of astilbe and sweet peas will make the arrangement feel as if you plucked all of these stems from your quaint garden in the English countryside.

FEATURING:

Darcey Bussell (page 122)

Stephen Rulo (page 186)

Distant Drums (page 84)

When it comes to classic garden colors, I think of a deep crimson red, a salmon-to-apricot blend, and a more neutral bloom that is more than meets the eye. Paired together in a vase, roses like Darcey Bussell, Stephen Rulo, and Distant Drums shift from one end of this color spectrum to the other.

MAINTAINING AND CARING FOR YOUR CUT ROSES

NOW THAT YOUR ROSES HAVE BEEN TRIMMED AND PLACED IN A vase, make sure they receive what they need to continue thriving. After they've been harvested from the plant, roses can last for multiple days if you practice some basic care to keep them happy each day. Once you've performed this care routine on your cut roses a few times, it will become second nature.

- Keep out of direct sun.

- Keep away from air-conditioning vents and wind.

- Maintain an indoor temperature of 65 to 70°F (18.3 to 21°C), if possible.

- Remove wilted flowers from your vessel as they die.

- Change the water every day, or every other day at the least.

- Add flower food (see recipe, below) when first creating the arrangement and every few days thereafter.

- Trim the ends of the roses every few days so water uptake continues.

FLOWER FOOD RECIPE

Combine 2 tablespoons (30 ml) lemon juice, 1 tablespoon (15 ml) sugar, and ½ teaspoon (2.5 ml) bleach in approximately 1 quart (1 L) water and add to your chosen vessel. The citric acid from the lemon juice will lower the pH in the vase, the sugar will provide nutrients to the stems, and the bleach will kill bacteria and prevent them from growing in the water.

CREATING A
ROSE-FILLED TABLESCAPE

WHEN YOU GROW ROSES AT HOME, YOU ALREADY HAVE THE MOST
beautiful décor in your own backyard. A spring afternoon can be more
magical with roses at your side, whether you're enjoying a meal with a friend
or family member or simply reading a good book.

Whether you have only thirty minutes to snip some roses from the garden
and throw them in a vase or enough time to layer your table with blooms—
from cakes to place settings and beyond—you won't regret incorporating
roses into your special get-togethers. Here's how I style a larger table for
more formal, memorable events.

- Keep the color palette of the event as loose as possible so you aren't
  pigeonholed into using one color of flower. I like to use mismatched
  vintage plates to encourage this breadth.

- Create multiple arrangements (as opposed to one large, central
  arrangement) similar in size and structure and run them down the
  length of the table. This ensures each of your guests has a beautiful,
  rose-filled view. Alternatively, mix groupings of roses in different
  sizes—from larger arrangements to bud vases—for a varied look.

- Layer the table with textures. In addition to my vintage plates, I use
  mismatched serving pieces, serveware with varying textures (like
  scalloped plates or hobnail bowls), and different vessels for the roses.
  This approach makes the table look informal but intentional at the
  same time. It's also a great way to incorporate items you've collected
  over the years.

- Add roses to the table beyond the vase. Cut blooms at the head and
  place them on a cake, on napkins, or simply scatter the flowers about
  the table.

CREATING A DREAMY FLORAL ARCH

A floral arch is a truly spectacular sight to see in the garden and can provide a splendid backdrop for special events and occasions. If you have plenty of roses to harvest and some determination, you can create your own floral arch using zip ties and chicken wire.

WHAT YOU'LL NEED

- Zip ties and/or paddle wire

- Chicken wire

- A garden arch or trellis

- Water tubes

- Moss

- Clippers

- Several bunches of green filler

- Several bunches of freshly harvested roses

- Several bunches of astilbe, ferns, or other structural flowers or foliage

STEP 1: Secure zip ties or wire to attach chicken wire to the structure. (You can use floral foam instead, but I try to practice more sustainable options with our roses.) Prepare water tubes for delicate flowers, and soak moss and nestle it inside the chicken wire.

STEP 2: Add your greenery base, filling in the entire frame with green filler. You can stick stems directly into chicken wire or attach greens to the structure using wire.

STEP 3: Add your flowers. Layer them in at different lengths to create dimension. Cluster your flower varieties together to mimic how flowers grow in nature. Keep adding flowers outward for depth.

STEP 4: Add in textural elements like astilbe or ferns to fill in any holes or cover mechanics that are showing.

ACKNOWLEDGMENTS

CREATING A BOOK THAT CAPTURES THE nuances of a living plant takes patience, precision, and vision. This project was years in the making and was touched by many people who made it come into bloom.

Georgianna Lane, Marcy Simpson, Keith Wintermute, and Jose Villa worked their magic to capture the roses you see in these pages through their beautiful photography.

Kelli Kehler helped to weave my words and thoughts into these pages and was also instrumental in project managing and styling our photo shoots.

I am grateful to Morgan Wynia for her gorgeous floral styling in this book, and for her support and friendship over the years.

To David Austin and his team, thank you for your steadfast partnership and for continuing to breed the loveliest English roses. It is an honor to grow them in our gardens.

Scott, Cindy, Andy, and Timmy Klittich of Otto and Sons Nursery have provided our farm with beautiful roses since 2016. We could never have grown our rose collection without them.

Thank you to Tyler Francis of Francis Roses for procuring and growing the best roses in the world for us.

I am also grateful to our breeders at Interplant, Tantau, Jan Spek Rozen, Georges Delbard, Schreurs, and NIRP for continuing their legacy of breeding excellence.

My agent, Judy Linden, helped me navigate this book process and ensure that it was crafted by the best possible team.

Thank you to my team at Artisan Books for your support and guidance: Bridget Monroe Itkin, Lia Ronnen, Laura Cherkas, Carol White, Diana Valcárcel, Annie O'Donnell, Suet Chong, Jane Treuhaft, Shubhani Sarkar, Nancy Murray, Donna Brown, Erica Huang, Zach Greenwald, Allison McGeehon, Theresa Collier, Brittany Dennison, and Amy Michelson.

I'm also thankful to E'Ana Bordon, my right hand at Grace Rose Farm, for her dedication to this book. Ridge Walker, thank you for wisdom and knowledge.

To all of our customers and followers of Grace Rose Farm, thank you for your loyalty.

Lastly, my deepest gratitude goes to my husband, Ryan, and our daughter, Seraphina.

And to you reading this book, may this be the moment when you, too, fall in love with roses and the joy of growing them.

PHOTOGRAPHY CREDITS

All photographs are by MARCY SIMPSON except for the following:

DAVID AUSTIN ROSES: pages 63, 106, 123, 139, 188

GEORGIANNA LANE: pages 4–5, 12, 14, 18, 26, 31, 39, 41, 44, 50, 51, 53, 60, 64, 66, 68, 71, 74, 77, 81, 89, 92, 95, 101, 107, 119, 120, 131, 143, 145, 154, 165, 169, 173, 179, 193, 197, 201, 209, 210, 265, 274, 276 (top), 278–279, 280

HOA BROTHERS: pages 32, 33, 54, 58, 90, 91, 124, 138, 148, 168, 189, 196

JOSE VILLA: pages 8, 266, 304

KEITH WINTERMUTE: pages 40, 47, 59, 72, 75, 82, 83, 86, 96, 99, 102, 112, 115, 125, 128, 159, 161, 174, 176, 184, 199, 208

SHUTTERSTOCK / FUGAZI IMAGES: page 252

SHUTTERSTOCK / MAREN WINTER: page 251

STAR® ROSES AND PLANTS: page 177

INDEX

GRACIELINDA POULSON is the founder of Grace Rose Farm, an estate in Southern California that grows and ships hundreds of rose varieties to florists and customers each year. Gracie has built a devoted base of rose-loving customers and fans, inspiring and empowering novice gardeners and green thumbs alike to begin their own rose journey in their home gardens. Grace Rose Farm has been featured in publications like *Martha Stewart Living*, *Country Living*, *Victoria*, and many more. Gracie, her husband, Ryan, and their daughter, Seraphina, live in Southern California, where they nurture their rose-growing passion each day. Follow along on Instagram at @gracerosefarm.